PIRATES of KEY WEST

HIGH TIMES ON THE HIGH SEAS IN THE ROARING 1980s

KELLY RYAN HARRIGER

SUNBURY PRESS

Mechanicsburg, PA USA

Published by Sunbury Press, Inc.
Mechanicsburg, PA USA

www.sunburypress.com

For information about special discounts for bulk purchases, please contact Sunbury Press Orders Dept. at (855) 338-8359 or orders@sunburypress.com.

To request one of our authors for speaking engagements or book signings, please contact Sunbury Press Publicity Dept. at publicity@sunburypress.com.

FIRST SUNBURY PRESS EDITION: January 2026

Set in Adobe Garamond | Interior design by Crystal Devine | Cover by Kelly Ryan Harriger | Edited by Gabrielle Kirk.

Publisher's Cataloging-in-Publication Data
Names: Harriger, Kelly Ryan, author.
Title: Pirates of Key West : high times on the high seas in the roaring 1980s / Kelly Ryan Harriger.
Description: First trade paperback edition. | Mechanicsburg, PA : Sunbury Press, 2026.
Summary: When offered a chance to be the skipper on a smuggling trip to Mexica, author Kelly Ryan Harriger jumped at the chance. Over the next two years, he took several more trips to Jamaica, got busted, and then switched to transporting cocaine around South Florida. When his lifestyle finally caught up to him, he was forced to walk away and start a new life.
Identifiers: ISBN : 979-8-88819-334-1 (softcover).
Subjects: TBA.

Designed in the USA
0 1 1 2 3 5 8 13 21 34 55

For the Love of Books!

For Suzy

CONTENTS

INTRODUCTION

Everything in this book really happened, and I've written it as best as I can remember it. Over the years, I experienced a lot of trepidation and anxiety every time I considered writing this story, because I still wasn't sure how I felt about my role in it, or how people who know me would respond. It happened over forty years ago, and during that time I rarely considered writing it down for these reasons. But within the past year, several friends suggested I tell this story. After some thought and checking with lawyers, I decided to move forward and not look back.

The statute of limitations on what I did is six years, and that passed by 1988. The bosses I worked for were in their late forties and early fifties, so they're either very old, or not with us anymore. I was arrested and stood trial for the last trip, but as you can't be tried for the same crime twice, I'm in safe water on that count because of double-jeopardy laws, according to Article 1, Section 9 of the Florida Constitution. Any physical evidence, I'm quite certain, went up in smoke before I ever went to trial. For obvious reasons the names have been changed to protect the identity of friends and the people I worked for, and specific details omitted. Despite the illegality of my adventures, I must confess that even if I knew then what I know now, I probably would have done it anyway. I have a few regrets, but no apologies. It's part of who I was at that time, but I haven't been that guy for a long, long time, so it's time to tell the story.

PROLOGUE

I'll be honest. I was worried, possibly even scared. At moments like these, right when a deal was supposed to go down, I was always thinking of the possibility of being shot, or stabbed, or tossed overboard to drown. I was a worst-case scenario guy, and when things went well, I felt lucky. It's not an unnatural feeling, considering the types of people I often worked with. I couldn't stop being worried. In less than an hour, the sailboat I was sitting in would be filled with a ton of high-grade Jamaican marijuana, and I'd be sailing back across the western Caribbean, around the tip of Cuba, and on to Florida while trying to get past the Coast Guard and the DEA without getting arrested. If I made it that far, I'd have to get that ton of weed off the boat somewhere in the Florida Keys without getting caught by the Florida Marine Patrol and the other law enforcement organizations they regularly worked with.

I'd done this successfully twice before, but on this trip, I'd had a bad feeling about everything, every step of the way. I checked my watch and kept an eye on the shoreline, focused on a small park with a public beach just one hundred yards away. After a few minutes, I saw the three green flashes and turned on our running lights so that whoever was on shore would know we'd seen their signal. It was just after dusk, and the sky was quickly turning dark.

We weighed anchor and slipped out of Discovery Bay, a small bay about 30 miles east of Montego Bay, on the north shore of Jamaica. It was an idyllic location, open to the Caribbean, but protected from swells by some shoals at the harbor's entrance. It was 1982, and tourists hadn't yet discovered it except as a stopover on the drive between Montego Bay and Ocho Rios. My crew, Greg and Pete, were close friends from Key West, and the three of us chatted about Discovery Bay being the sort of place where you'd retire and live the island life. The green mountains stood behind the town, mostly small, modest homes, and the clucks and bleats of chickens and goats rose from the hillside above us. The entire area had a laid-back, sleepy feel, and it almost felt like paradise.

We were a bit nervous about the pickup that evening, because there'd be none of the people we normally worked with. We'd be meeting a crew made up entirely of local Jamaican gangs, who'd deliver the 2,000 pounds of high-grade weed on the skiffs. The people I worked for would then meet other members of the gang in Miami to pay them for the load, which we were getting on credit. At that point in the trade, Jamaican drug gangs hadn't yet adopted the Mexican and Colombian habit of collecting the money at the point of purchase. They'd learned that they could quickly get into the lucrative marijuana trade by offering their product on credit, to be paid for upon delivery in the USA.

This point alone made us a bit more comfortable than we'd been on our first trip, which was to Alvarado, Mexico, where we dealt with the Mexican cartel. We knew that the Jamaican guys weren't going to mess with us or cause any problems until they got paid. This was a different business model than the one used by the Mexicans and Colombians, where cash rip-offs were common among low-level dealers, who were fine making a quick buck over developing long-term business dealings.

After spotting the green light blinking in three-burst successions—our GO signal from shore—we motored out of the harbor beyond the break-water, dropped anchor, and waited.

Within twenty minutes, we heard outboard motors approaching us in the dark. We'd sailed from Montego Bay a day earlier but avoided spending too much time ashore in Discovery Bay to avoid questions from the locals, who already suspected why we were there. It's not that sailboats were an uncommon sight, but a sailboat with just three men on it was something they'd seen before, and most locals knew we weren't there on vacation. We had a few curious skiffs with young men come by our 42' Tartan sloop during the day, and the occupants would smile and wave, and cruise on by. They knew. We were just worried how many others knew as well.

I was nervous this trip, but I was the captain. It was part of my job to be worried and vigilant. It was my third smuggling trip, and I felt a sense of dread come over me every now and then, a foreboding that this one wouldn't be a walk in the park like the last one, or a comedy of errors like the first one.

On the trip down around the tip of Cuba, while tacking toward the Cayman Islands, we'd been buzzed by a low-flying twin engine aircraft, the same type commonly flown by the DEA. The airplane had been flying toward us, at several thousand feet, but upon seeing us, banked steeply a few miles behind us, dropped down to water level, and came up on us from behind. We could see someone in the airplane taking photos as they came up on our stern just a few hundred feet above the surface of the ocean. There was no good reason to do that unless you wanted to get the name of the boat, which is clearly what they were doing. My first clue that this wouldn't go as planned.

My second clue came upon docking in Montego Bay, at the Montego Bay Yacht club, when we were visited by Customs during our check-in. Our last trip to Jamaica, just months earlier, had been on the same boat, and we'd made the mistake of not clearing Customs before getting our load and heading back to the States. We now found ourselves trying to enter Customs while technically still being in Jamaican waters, as we'd never officially left them during the last trip a few months earlier.

When the Customs officer arrived, I could clearly see he was nervous, and I'd soon find out why. We didn't have any exit papers from Miami, as we didn't want US Customs to know where we were headed, but it wasn't uncommon to just sail into port from another island without them, so he wasn't upset by that fact. When he started talking, he cut right to the point.

"You are here to get permission to sail Jamaican waters?"

"Yes," I replied.

"This is your first time here?"

I sensed a trap being set, and I didn't lie.

"No, sir. We were here just a few months ago."

"I see. On this vessel?"

"Yes, sir. On this vessel."

"Answer me this, sir," he said. "Why do you need me to grant you permission to sail these waters when you never left them? I have no record of you leaving from the last time you were here."

At that point, I understood his nervousness. He was trying to catch me in a contradiction, and fortunately, I didn't concoct a story that I'd have to wiggle out of later. I needed to think fast.

"Oh, that. I forgot about that. You see, we were up the coast and got word of an emergency and needed to get back to the States as quickly as possible. I didn't realize it would cause any problems."

I could tell he knew better, and I was fairly certain that he knew why we were there. I was also certain he dealt with smugglers all the time, and since no crime was being committed by simply arriving on the island, he could only look the other way.

"Here's what I'm going to do." He was orderly and precise, both in his mannerism and dress. He gestured as he spoke, with a professorial intensity, and his crisply pressed ivory shirt gave him the look of an upper-class islander of good heritage. It was clear the job gave him status, and he was proud of it, even at his level. After talking with Greg, Pete, and Garry, our backer and financier from Miami, we decided that if push came to shove, we'd just bribe him. In my experience, that's one thing that always seemed to work. In the Caribbean, every official seemed to have a price.

Push did come to shove. Our Customs officer was going to go by the book and not just turn his back. He requested a formal, written explanation, in extreme detail, explaining how we arrived at our situation. If he was going to allow us back into Jamaican waters and close the books on our last visit, he needed to have the documentation to do so. The job fell to me, as the captain, to write up the explanation for departing without clearing customs on our last trip, and why we were back again so soon. He clearly wanted to cover his ass, and so he requested the detailed explanation. He would return in the evening to pick it up and would decide our fate at that time. Shortly after he left, I sat down, poured a glass of some fine Haitian rum, and spent the remainder of the afternoon writing the most wonderful work of fiction I'd composed to date, leaving out no details, and offering way more than he asked for.

He returned that evening, looking more official than ever. He was carrying a soft leather briefcase as he walked down the dock and was wearing a shiny silver watch that might have been a Rolex but was probably a knockoff. High-quality fake Rolexes were common bribes, as the good fakes were still expensive watches that passed for the real deal, but cost about a tenth of the cost of a real Rolex. He boarded the boat and sat down in the galley. We were all present, including the women who'd sailed down with us, and we crowded around him as he read the explanation in its entirety. When he was done, he laid it on the table, took off his glasses, and declared, "This is satisfactory. We will proceed with your entry papers."

We were all relieved, and after the paperwork was done and he stepped to the dock, we noticed Garry had followed him and had walked down the dock with him. We saw them shake hands, watched as the Customs officer looked at his hand (there was something in it), and then nervously turned his back toward the marina so that he was facing us. He continued to talk to Garry, and appeared nervous, but then parted and walked away quickly. Garry returned to the boat with a smile.

"What was that all about?" I asked.

"I gave him five hundred bucks. That's probably more cash than he makes in a month at that job. He protested just enough, but still took it, so I'm guessing it's not the first time he's been bribed. I think we're good. I even got his name and card and told him we'd ask for him by name next time."

I'm sure the customs officer took that last exchange as more of a softly veiled threat than a compliment. In any case, the exchange rate was about 1:3 in those days, so our local customs officer had just scored about $1,500 Jamaican for a few hours' work. That was a lot of money for a public servant in 1982.

We were now in the country officially and safe, free to sail Jamaican waters. But the confrontation made me nervous, because I also knew that the DEA talked to these guys and picked their brains for anomalies like our situation. Fortunately, we were informed by a Jamaican gang member on our earlier trip that the DEA was rather cheap in the bribery department, so we were one-up on them in the flow of information. But the situation was still another red flag. Another reason to be paranoid, and I knew I wasn't wrong about this feeling of dread.

When we heard the approaching outboard motors, I had my crew get in position. I had the lee side of the sailboat lined with large white rubber fenders to protect the hull as we bobbed in the swells, and we tied up the first skiff while the second sat just downwind of us, idling the engine just enough not to drift away. Typically, there'd be a guy or two on the skiffs handing bales to another guy straddling the two boats, who'd hand bales to me, which I'd pass down through the hatch to my crew, who'd then start stacking the bales in the cabin. Our sailboat was only 42 feet, so 2,000 pounds of weed took up a lot of space. We always kept the bow bunks open, to keep the bow light, and put the bulk of the bales near the beam, the widest part of the sailboat, and then stashed the remainder in the two smaller stern bunks that went under the cockpit area.

A full boat didn't leave a lot of room to get around below deck, but we didn't need much space. The women who'd come down with us were already on an airliner home, taking our film and cameras with them. We took lots of photos of our trip down, but never, ever took any of our actual operation. If you're going to smuggle, you don't document your actions on film. Once the boat was loaded, the skiffs usually took off immediately and headed for shore. But the last boat didn't untie this time. I was confused, even more so when a man on the skiff climbed onto the sailboat and sat down in the cockpit.

I looked at the man who seemed to be the leader of the group. Standing up beside him was a man I'd spoken to a few days earlier up in the mountains. He held a large package, wrapped in a garbage bag, and taped with duct tape. I nodded at them.

"What's up?"

He pointed at the man sitting in the cockpit. "This is Muggy. He go back with you."

"I wasn't told about this. Who made this decision?" I wasn't happy with this development at all.

"Your boss man. He make that decision. Part of our agreement. He stays with the shipment until we get paid."

"I don't think we have enough food for four people. We didn't plan for this."

"Muggy don't eat much. He be fine. Catch some fish or something."

I didn't know what to do. I didn't want to argue with a Jamaican gang member who had a gun in his waistband, and if Garry had made a deal for us to carry a gang member to Miami, then I guess I was stuck with that decision. But now I was not only looking at smuggling charges if caught, but also human trafficking. I was really getting a bad, bad feeling about this trip.

"Okay. I guess that's that."

"Okay. Have a safe trip. Cool runnings." He sat back down in the skiff.

But I wasn't finished. I still had some business to conduct on my own. I nodded to the man holding the package. He handed it to me, and I handed him the five one-hundred-dollar bills in my pocket. He'd insisted on US dollars and had specifically requested that I not pay him in Jamaican money. I took the package and laid it in the cockpit. I shook hands with him, our deal finished. That package was my personal guarantee of a payday to cover my ass if this deal went badly back in the States.

Once our business was done, he climbed onto the skiff, and they motored away. And that was that.

There we sat, still at anchor, catching our breath after loading and stowing two thousand pounds of weed, and pondering the fact that we now had another passenger, a Jamaican gang member, to transport with the shipment. This was not going as smoothly as I'd hoped.

After a quick rest, we pulled anchor, raised the jib and mainsail, turned the boat around, and set a course due west for the Yucatan Channel, where we'd turn north for a bit, then northeast and back into US waters. As we worked, Muggy didn't say a word. We didn't talk to him, either. We didn't know what to say, and it was clear none of us felt like making small talk. We had no idea what to expect in the week ahead when we'd be returning to US waters, and my sense of dread only grew worse.

But I'm getting way ahead of myself here. Let's back up a bit and start at the beginning.

ONE

CHILDHOOD DREAMS

I never set out to be a smuggler. It wasn't a dream or a life goal when I was young, and the thought never entered my mind until I was in my twenties. I did, however, want to be a sailor since I'd been a young boy. My father was a military office and base commander, and we'd lived in Hawaii and Florida for years when I was in grade school, and it's where I fell in love with the ocean and island life. Dad was stationed at Hickam AFB near Honolulu, but didn't want to live on base or have his kids go to base school, so he rented a house on the North Shore of Oahu, just east of Haleiwa, right on the shore along the Kamehameha Highway. It was an idyllic spot to grow up, and my folks loved spending time with their local friends as much as their Air Force family. My brother and sisters loved it as well. We lived right on the beach, with a beautiful view of Kaena Point, and we attended a local elementary school where we were the only haoles in the classes, largely a mix of locals, Japanese, Chinese, and Filipino kids. My father became good friends with the Japanese-American owners of the Sea View Inn, which sat right next to the Anahulu Bridge. He took me there often, and it's where I had my first sushi and sashimi, right off the fishing boats.

My father loved being in tight with the locals, and our family was always invited to all their luaus and hukilaus. It was an exciting life for a grade-school boy, made all the better by the fishing trips in small skiffs with my father's friends. I found myself completely in love with the ocean from that point on, and other than a brief one-year stint at Lackland AFB in San Antonio, Texas, we were right back on the water again when my father was assigned to a small Air Force unit on Cudjoe Key in the Florida Keys that focused on visual intelligence gathering, primarily Cuba and the Straits of Florida. This would be his last assignment before retiring, and for those two years I soaked up the sun and spent as much time on boats as I possibly could. I lived for the weekends and the opportunity to be somewhere on the ocean, away from everyone. The ocean is where I found my peace, and I never wanted to leave.

After two years living in the Florida Keys, my father finally retired, and we returned to his boyhood home in rural western Pennsylvania, which was a shock to a bunch of kids who'd been raised on the ocean and around subtropical weather for most of their young lives. But it was a new adventure, and we were up to the challenges of living on a working farm with animals, farm equipment, and snow (for the first time in our lives that we could remember). I didn't think much about the ocean for the first few years after moving to Pennsylvania, but that all changed when I picked up an issue of National Geographic and found the first of several installments about a young man named Robin Lee Graham, who had set out from California on a 24-foot Lapworth sloop to become the youngest person to circumnavigate the globe on a sailboat.

I was instantly captured by the story, and kept that issue by my bedside, where I'd thumb through it regularly, looking at the photos I'd already looked at hundreds of times. I could close my eyes and feel myself back on the ocean, this time on my own boat, at anchor in some tropical port, living in swim trunks and flip-flops, which is what I always wore on my own time during my earlier years on the ocean. The magic of those photos never faded, and it fueled my dreams of returning to the ocean someday. National Geographic carried his story in several installments over three years, and I saved every issue, reading the stories and looking at the photos over and over. Few things in my young life captured my imagination as powerfully as those stories and photos, and I began to read more books dealing with seafaring and sailing. While still in high school, and years before I'd set foot on a boat again, I was already reading books on navigation and learning how to use a sextant. When my opportunity came, I wanted to be ready to go at full speed. While I entertained dreams of sailing around the world, I was prepared to settle for something less ambitious, such as sailing the Caribbean. My real goal was just to find a way to be back on the ocean, on a sailboat, living a life I'd dreamed about for years. I would get that chance, but not in a way that I ever could have dreamed up at that point in my life.

My plans after high school were to go to college, specifically an art school, but my father had other plans. He'd always insisted that my brother and I should go into the Air Force, do our four years, and then, if we wanted to go to college, we could use the GI Bill and save him some money. When I rejected that idea and got accepted at an art college in Pittsburgh, he told me I was on my own and that I could pay for it myself. I didn't know what to do, but as my sister had since moved back to Key West, I decided to head back there myself. After hanging around my hometown of Brookville for the summer, which consisted of smoking weed and riding dirt bikes almost every day, I packed a small duffel bag with some clothes—literally everything I owned at that point—bought a ticket on a Trailways bus for Key West and took off one night from the bus station in Punxsutawney. It was an uneventful ride, except for my arrival, as I hadn't told my sister I was coming. She was living with her boyfriend in a tiny studio apartment and clearly didn't have room for me. I hung around for about a month, found a job bussing tables at the local IHOP, and after a few weeks got the grand idea that I would go to California and make something of myself. I hadn't worked out the details, but I figured I'd work that part out later when I arrived and got settled down.

I assumed that I'd be able to make a lot more money in California and that it would be a perfect place to buy a sailboat. I was still seventeen and naïve, still filled with a sense of wonder, and my lack of situational awareness hadn't developed yet. I was literally at the whim of every shiny idea that floated in front of me, and I found a special joy in chasing every one of them. This character flaw would play an important role in what was about to take place a few years later.

As I hitchhiked up the Keys, I encountered another hitchhiker leaving Key West. He was considerably older than me, probably in his 40s, and was the wildest hippie I'd ever met. He was dressed like an Indian holy man (which seemed odd for a man named Dwayne), with a walking stick and a large hemp shoulder bag that held all his belongings. He had long, wild, frizzy hair and talked about the craziest things—things I'd never thought of or encountered in my own cerebral ramblings. I was fascinated by him, but also a bit concerned. Not frightened, just concerned, primarily because of his crazy energy, something I'd never experienced before. We got rides together throughout the day, and when night fell, we were somewhere around Fort Lauderdale, so we hung around a McDonald's parking lot until it closed and then slept in the bushes nearby. The next morning, we were back on the road, back on I-95 and heading north to destinations unknown.

Dwayne had friends in Saint Augustine and told me I was welcome to crash there for another night. After a long day of hitchhiking, we arrived in Saint Augustine late in the evening and found our way to his friend's house. It was a night I'll never forget. I was seventeen, fresh out of high school in rural western Pennsylvania, and found myself in a house filled with hippies, drugs, and alcohol. It was wilder than any anti-drug movie I'd seen in high school, and I wanted to experience everything I'd ever been instructed to stay away from. I smoked hash, took some peyote, and drank just about anything that was put in front of me. If there was a downside, I don't remember it. Even when I found myself with the spins, I enjoyed the wild ride until they went away.

Over the course of the evening, I discovered that I was the life of the party, and all those seasoned hippies were having a great time introducing the young farm kid to their lifestyle. And then something amazing happened, and it's a moment that was one of the many turning points in my life. Oliver Wendell Holmes once stated that once your mind is stretched by a new idea, it will never again return to its original size. Steve Jobs was once asked what made his vision at Apple so different from Bill Gates's vision at Microsoft, and Steve commented that Bill Gates had never done mind-expanding drugs, and that made all the difference in their opposing visions. Looking back from my current viewpoint, I must agree with both statements. For better or worse, mind-expanding drugs alter your thinking forever. They literally seem to create a vacuum in your mind that must be filled, and you begin to think and create in ways never imagined, satisfying a fresh yearning to better understand everything. That's what happened to me that night. I found myself wanting to know everything about everything, and I wouldn't rest until I'd filled my life with every possible experience.

We were still going strong at daybreak, and over a breakfast of eggs and Cuban coffee, I was introduced to the Ram Dass classic *Be Here Now*, which had been released just a few years earlier, and had quickly become the seeking hippie's ultimate guide to understanding the journey of life and all the mysticism it entailed. I was fascinated by the book and sat in the morning Saint Augustine sun in someone's backyard, stoned beyond all reasonable measures, reading a book about the expanded mind on Life's journey. I knew I had to have a copy and promised myself to purchase one as soon as I had money and was living somewhere stable.

One line stood out that day and became one of the many mantras of my life. It was a simple statement, but profound in its wisdom: "When you know how to listen, everybody is the guru." That simple sentence, in one stroke, changed my perspective on living, and from that point forward, I found myself always trying my best to pay attention to people I encountered, no matter who they might be or their station in life. It's not easy in this distracting world, but it's an action that will change your life and make you less self-absorbed.

By late morning, I was starting to clear my head and was anxious to get back on the road to California, but I now had a new vision, based upon my experiences during the night. I now decided that I was going to hitchhike around the world with nothing but a passport and some clothes, letting myself be blown along by the winds of fortune, going wherever my heart desired, or maybe even led against my better judgment. I wanted to embrace everything. Soak it all in. I wanted Life in giant bites, as much as I could chew, and I was starting right that moment. I said my goodbyes to my new friends, thanked them for their hospitality, and found my way back to Highway 1, then back to I-95, and then I-10 west and parts unknown. It was a bright, warm afternoon, and the glare hurt my eyes. I was wearing a pair of leather sandals, a pair of khaki shorts, and a t-shirt. My duffle bag held a pair of shoes, more shorts, a pair of jeans, a few t-shirts, and a toothbrush and toothpaste. That was everything I owned in the entire world, and I was excited as I started my journey around the world. I kept repeating that to myself throughout the afternoon—"I'm going around the world"—and it felt magnificent. I'd become a different person overnight. My experience had unlocked something within me.

The trip through the Florida panhandle was uneventful. I don't remember much about the rides, other than I seemed to be getting a lot of rides from well-meaning folks who seemed worried about me and kept reminding me to be careful. It occurred to me years later that they probably thought I was a teen runaway, and I'm sure I looked the part.

Somewhere between Mobile, Alabama, and Baton Rouge, Louisiana, I was picked up by a young man in an old pickup truck who had a birthday cake on the front seat. He was dressed like a cowboy, with an old-style Tom Mix Stetson hat. He looked like a working cowboy and introduced himself as Pepper. No other name, just Pepper, which I assumed had to be a nickname, or possibly a last name. He was very quiet, but not in a way that made me nervous. He struck me as a man at peace, who just wasn't into small talk. He asked me where I was heading, and I told him I was heading around the world. He didn't laugh but instead asked where I was heading in the immediate future.

"I'm just living on the road for now," I told him.

"When was the last time you ate?" he asked.

"I don't remember. Yesterday, I think." I didn't remember being hungry, so I didn't care about food.

"I don't have much money, but would you like a piece of cake?"

I was surprised. He'd mentioned earlier that he was on his way to his daughter's birthday party with the cake. I was confused that he was asking me if I wanted a piece of his daughter's cake before she'd even seen it or blown out the candles. I was humbled by his offer and said no. I couldn't imagine how his daughter would react to seeing a piece of her cake missing, and I didn't want to be the cause of that.

We were on Interstate 10, and when he got to his exit, he pulled over, opened the cake, pulled out a Buck knife and cut me a large piece of the cake while I protested. He cut a piece of cardboard from the cake box and put the cake on it before handing it to me. I was standing beside the truck with the passenger door open, and I took the cake and thanked him before he drove away. It was an act of kindness I remember to this day, because it was so simple and extraordinary. I remember eating the cake and crying, and I couldn't figure out why. I felt like an idiot and walked away from the Interstate ramp, tears in my eyes and confused by the experience. It took me years to understand that I was reacting to the act of someone with a pure, loving, unencumbered soul, someone kind enough to give me a piece of his daughter's birthday cake to make sure I didn't go hungry. I vowed I'd never forget his name, and I'm telling his story here. If you want to be like anyone, be like Pepper, a man who defined his nature with a simple act of kindness when he had no obligation to do so.

As I made my way into Texas, I passed through Houston, and then up through the state with the intention of visiting my aunt, uncle, and cousins in Lubbock, up in the Panhandle region. I'd just seen them earlier in the summer at the family farm in Pennsylvania, where they came every summer, and it just seemed natural to pop in and say hello. I was developing a bad habit of just popping in everywhere to say hello and never providing any warning.

I arrived in Lubbock and got dropped off at a gas station on Avenue Q, found a payphone, and contacted my surprised cousin, who came and picked me up. At their home, my surprised but amused uncle asked me what I was up to, and where I was going.

"Around the world," I told him.

He laughed, caught off guard by my answer. "Do you have a job or money?" he asked.

"No."

"How far do you plan to go without a job or money?"

"All the way. I made it this far without any."

"Well, I'll make you an offer. If you'd like to stay here and work for a bit, you're welcome to. If you still want to go around the world, that's your decision. But if you'd like to stay and save some money and go to college, you're welcome to get your start here."

I didn't even think about it, but then I didn't give much thought to anything in those days, and typically just flew by the seat of my pants minute to minute. It just struck me as a fun turn in my plans, and I quickly said yes. I found a job at a car wash a week later, started saving money for a full year while becoming a resident, and started at Texas Tech the following fall, with my plans for traveling the world on hold for the time being. I didn't know how long I'd go to college, or how long I'd stay in Lubbock, but I was happy for the moment and didn't give it much thought. At that point in my life, I rarely had plans beyond a day.

It was during this time that I fell in love with the early music of Jimmy Buffett, the poet laureate of the Florida Keys and the sailing life. His early albums were filled with beautiful songs about the ocean, and particularly the sailing life. One song that really caught my attention was "A Pirate Looks at Forty," a song about a sailor who'd spent some time smuggling weed, and made enough money to "buy Miami, but pissed it away so fast." I loved that song, and it reignited my desire to sail, but with a new goal in mind. I wanted to be a modern-day pirate, and I dreamed of returning to the Keys, getting into sailing, getting a chance to make a few runs, buying a sailboat, and living a life on the seas with my dream woman, who was still out there somewhere.

Life has other plans, though, and I met a different woman, fell in love, and decided to stay as long as the relationship worked. Barbara was my first real love, and we loved each other madly, as you can only do when you're experiencing that first real love. There's a sense of abandon, of not caring about anything else, and knowing the other person felt the same way about you. It was an intense relationship between two immature, overly-emotional hotheads, with its share of ups and downs, but none of it seemed to matter. We couldn't stay away from each other. It felt like we were made for each other and just had to work out the details and grow up a bit. We were two individuals who loved our personal freedom, but also loved each other, and the relationship had long stretches of peace and tranquility, interspersed with spells of upheaval and impulsiveness. Over time, things settled down as we found an uneasy equilibrium, but chaos was always lurking nearby, and we had to work to avoid it. Looking back from my current perspective, I think there was a part of both of us that enjoyed the drama and felt it added to the attraction we had for each other.

Over the years, we maintained an on-again, off-again relationship, each briefly dating others, but always finding a way to return to each other, where we shared an uncommon bond that we could not seem to break. Some might consider this an unhealthy relationship, but that would be a dismissive and incorrect assessment. It was simply a case of the right people at the wrong time, and we were both too immature to deal with an attraction so powerful. Had we given it time, I'm sure it would have matured, but other circumstances arose, and the course of my life changed once more.

As noted, I was anxious to return to Florida and dreamed about it often. I impulsively took off one winter with a friend over Christmas break and arrived in Key West intent on starting a new life there, but it was the dead of winter, the tourists were in town, and jobs and apartments were hard to find. Within a week or two, I bailed out, returned to Pennsylvania for the winter, and then decided to return to Lubbock again in the spring and give college and Barbara another try.

But once again, fate intervened in my life in the form of an old high school friend, who was living the life of a vagabond, drifting around the country wherever the winds of fortune blew him. At that time, they blew him into Lubbock, where he stayed for several weeks at my apartment. I expressed my dream of returning to the Keys to live and work on boats, and he made me an offer I couldn't refuse. If I drove him to Florida, he'd pay for everything and make sure I had enough to get set up in Key West. I couldn't refuse the offer, so in the spring we loaded up my old Volkswagen van and headed for Florida. I was determined to stay this time, and I told myself I was going to make it work no matter what. After a long, eventful journey through the Deep South with extended stays in New Orleans and Orlando, we finally arrived in Key West. What took place along the way could fill another book, but it would be too easy to get sidetracked by telling that story now, so I'll save it for another time.

TWO

KEY WEST

Once settled in Key West, I immediately found a job driving a tour train for tourists. I lived in my van in Boyd's Campground on Stock Island for several months after arriving and eventually found more permanent lodging when I moved into an apartment up the Keys with an exotic dancer who said she needed a roommate. She had a boyfriend, which I found strange, but I ignored my better judgment and moved in anyway. Everything seemed fine for a few months, until I returned home one day to find a Sheriff's car in the driveway. I was met by the Sheriff, who told me I wasn't allowed in the house. I couldn't figure out what was going on and was confused. It seemed the dancer had told them I was living there without any rental or lease agreement, so I'd have to move. I tried to reason with her, but I could tell she had no interest in talking to me, and I quickly realized I was being scammed and had been all along. She just wanted my possessions, and she was about to get them. The sheriff told me that I was not allowed in the house, even though all my possessions were there. I owned a lot of electronics, including a very expensive stereo system and my considerable record collection, as well as a Martin guitar. She brought out a small sack of my clothes, which was all I was allowed to have, and I was sent on my way by the Sheriff, who told me I could file a claim with the common pleas court if I wanted to contest the situation. I decided on the spot that I didn't want to do it, so I walked away from the situation with nothing but a bag of clothes again, and my van. I moved back to Boyd's Campground, where I lived for another few months until I saved some money and found a roommate in residential Key West, over on Flagler Avenue, just blocks from the eastern shore of the island. Stability at last. At that point, I finally felt like my life was about to begin.

A few months after moving to my new apartment, I remember walking down a back street, through a local neighborhood of old Conch cottages, feeling the night breeze on my face, and experiencing my entire body swell with the energy of the place. I was twenty-two at the time but felt as though my life was just beginning. It felt like home, a place I was always meant to be. I even remember that as I stood at the intersection of White and Petronia streets, I looked up at the sky, took a deep breath of everything around me, and smiled. At that moment, my life felt perfect, the fulfillment of a dream and what I hoped would become a pivotal point in my life. What happened from that point would be entirely up to me, and I wanted to make those dreams come true. I only wish now that I'd also thought about what I would do afterward. There's always an afterward, but I didn't realize it at the time. How you deal with the afterward can define a person more than the experience that came before.

The following few years brought a lot of change and shake-ups. I made friends with people who had boats, and we spent many days at the reef diving and spearfishing, and many a weekend camping in the backcountry, as it was called, an area filled with small mangrove islands, some with land mass and beaches, on the western side of the Keys. During those years I worked as a cab driver, a cook at Sloppy Joe's, and a bartender at The Half Shell Raw bar, where I was the night manager for the original owners, the Hargraves. I lived for partying, and the bars in Key West stayed open late. My mornings were spent nursing hangovers, sipping Cuban coffee, and playing my new guitar in the backyard. My days were spent on the beach, or running, and I'm convinced to this day that running and exercising were probably what kept me alive and relatively healthy despite all the drinking and drugs I was doing very regularly. No matter what, I was a dedicated runner who regularly put in four or five miles almost every other day. It seemed to create a balance to my life, and most likely kept me from bad health.

Sometime during my second year on the island, I finally got a job that put me closer to my dream. I landed a job as a first mate on a charter fishing boat, one that specialized in shark and deep wreck fishing over the more popular trolling boats that went out into the Gulfstream. The best part of my new job was our well-heeled clientele, who'd regularly charter the boat for two- and three-day fishing trips to the Dry Tortugas, a small archipelago about 80 miles west of Key West, which was home to Fort Jefferson, one of the coastal Martello forts in the Keys, and famous for holding Dr. Samuel Mudd as a prisoner after his capture for his involvement with John Wilkes Boothe.

I loved my life as a first mate and fell in love with the sea all over again. I worked throughout the winter months without a day off, sometimes working for over a month straight without a break. I was paid in cash and went to work at daybreak every day, returning home often after dark and piling my cash in a drawer in my bedroom. It was easy to save money, as I was too tired during the tourist season to go out, so the cash piled up. Finally, when spring rolled around and the charters began to become less common, I had some time to myself.

During this time in my life, I lived on Margaret Street in a tiny apartment in an older section of town that was primarily home to people of Cuban ancestry. There was a popular Cuban restaurant, La Lechonera, right on my corner, and I often ate breakfast and dinner there rather than cooking my own meals. I was flush with cash, and I only had to walk about 100 feet. One of my favorite meals for dinner was picadillo, a simple dish of ground meat with seasonings, some fried plantains, black beans, yellow rice, and Cuban bread, followed by flan for dessert. I think it was $1.75 for the picadillo plate, and another $.50 for the flan. Not a bad meal for three dollars, which included the tip.

My work as a first mate soon led to another dream job, this time working as crew on a tall ship from Newport, Rhode Island. The ship was a replica of the fast frigate used by Commander John Paul Jones in the Revolutionary War for attacks on the British. The replica ship was a faithful reproduction, right down to its cannons, which we fired regularly to the delight of the tourists. The ship spent the winter in Key West, setting sail twice a day in peak season, and we stayed busy seven days a week, just like the charter fishing boats. In Key West, you make money when it's there to be made, and during the peak of the winter season, you can stay as busy as you want to, as the business is there every single day.

I absolutely loved working on the tall ship and was soon scampering around up the rigging and running around on the yardarms of the square topsail. I had the confidence of a monkey, and completely trusting my abilities to function in the rigging at sea, went aloft every chance I got. There was something magical about being up in the rigging of a tall ship when it was under sail, and I couldn't get enough of it. The job became my identity, and I felt like a sailor at last. When I look back at the photos I took during that time in my life, I see myself at possibly the happiest point in my life, someone completely in love with what they were doing, and wanting to do nothing else with their life other than live in the moment and squeeze everything I could out of every day, days hopefully spent on the water.

Working on the tall ship would lead me to an opportunity to become a smuggler, although I didn't realize it at the time. On one of our twice-daily sailing trips, I met a wild character who seemed larger than life, almost a caricature. This guy's name was Mark. He also seemed like someone who exaggerated a lot, who might be stretching the truth a bit. He also seemed like a decent guy, but not necessarily one you'd trust with your life savings. He dressed like a character right out of a movie, with a Panama hat, wild Hawaiian shirts, white linen slacks and loafers, and carried himself with the air of someone who may or may not be abusing substances but certainly acted like he was. All that, and he liked to let on that he "knew" people, was well-connected, and had a steady supply of cocaine. The latter was one way to make lots of short-term friends in Key West. If you met someone who seemed to have access to lots of cocaine, you cultivated that friendship in the hopes that you'd get a bump or two. Everyone, it seemed, loved coke in those days, and it was the drug of choice and quite plentiful in Key West in the 1980s.

Mark and I chatted a lot on the trip that day, and he asked a lot of questions about my sailing experience, if I knew how to navigate, where I'd been on boats, and if I had a passport. He said he worked for a guy who liked to sail in the Caribbean and might be looking for some crew down the road. I was instantly intrigued and gave him my contact information, thinking this might be my big chance to sail in the Caribbean at last. After the sail, I walked over to Billie's Bar, right in the heart of old Key West on Front

Street, and we chatted more about sailing. As it turned out, he hadn't done much sailing himself, but was interested in learning more. I told him for the hundredth time how interested I was in crewing for his boss and told him to be sure to contact me if he needed anyone. He hung around Key West for another few days, took a second cruise with us, and departed the Island.

When spring rolled around, it was time for the Providence to pack up and head north to its regular berth just south of Newport, Rhode Island, at Fort Adams. The Providence spent the warmer summer months doing much the same thing there as it did in Key West, working as a floating, functioning museum at Fort Adams State Park. The ship needed crew to return, and I quickly agreed to make the trip. To raise some additional money, the captain was selling passage tickets to six people, who'd live and work on the ship with the crew on the journey up the coast. One of the people who signed up for the trip was Mark, who expressed a wish to learn about ocean-going life and work on a sailing vessel. Most of the crew knew him well by then, and we were all happy to have him aboard, even if we felt he'd be an unreliable mate. He was certainly an affable character, and entertaining to a fault, but I don't think anyone felt he'd have our backs if the chips were down in a rough situation, and we didn't want to have to test that theory, either.

The trip up the coast took about a month, with multiple planned stops in several major cities, where we did some day cruises for tourists, and for the first time since signing on as crew, I got to experience life aboard a tall ship on the open sea. It was an incredible experience, and we sailed up the coast with stops in Fort Lauderdale, Jacksonville, Savannah, Beaufort, and Charleston before setting out for Newport News, where we'd be docked near the *Calypso*, the research vessel used by the Cousteau Society led by Jacques Cousteau. But the trip to Newport News wasn't without incident. After leaving Charleston, we plotted a course past the Outer Banks in North Carolina, famous as a graveyard of shipwrecks due to a combination of poor navigation, unmapped shoals, and bad weather. Until this point in our trip, we had been treated to overall great weather and clear sailing. Our luck was about to change, with nearly disastrous results.

As we made our way around Frying Pan Shoals at the southernmost point of the Outer Banks, we learned we'd be heading into a major storm.

Although the ship was seaworthy, the captain felt it was taking an unnecessary risk to stay at sea in a tall ship with gun ports and a low deck. We'd been in some mild weather before, and it wasn't uncommon for waves to pound through the gun ports, even when closed, and have the lower deck awash with water. Because we were carrying paying passengers, it was decided that we'd pull into one of the many inlets that line the Outer Banks. It was already dark, and the captain requested a Coast Guard escort.

Having served as a former Naval Officer, and currently being the captain of a tall ship, he was certain they'd make themselves available as an escort through the narrow, shifting shoals that led into the port. I can't recall the name of the inlet, but it wasn't a heavily incorporated area and was primarily a port for commercial fishing boats and other large trawlers.

The Coast Guard came through and sent out a small cutter and escort vessel to guide us in through the channel, which took several hard turns and had sandy shoals on both sides. The swells were high, and although the Providence was running under diesel power and moving slowly, it began to surf on the incoming swells as we started down the narrow channel. The situation quickly went from concerning to downright dangerous, as we had little control over the ship when it began to surf down the front of the swells. All we could do as crew was try to keep the ship pointed in the right direction to avoid turning sideways in the swells, but by doing so, we couldn't follow the exact path of the channel. We all sensed something bad was about to happen when we saw the smaller, more maneuverable Coast Guard cutter take a tight turn in the channel, and we couldn't follow. We heard the captain of the cutter on the radio shouting for us to turn, but we simply couldn't—the ship was too big and cumbersome to make the tight turn while being picked up by a swell at the same time, but we didn't have any choice, so the captain tried to match the turn of the cutter. It was a case of being damned if you do, damned if you don't. If we hadn't tried to turn, we'd have run straight aground, bow first, into the sandy shoal to our lee. When we did turn, the ship went broadside to the waves and the swell, and we rocked over sideways, the yardarms swinging wildly, as the ship was picked up by the swells and dropped heavily to the sandy shoal, where it landed with a shudder.

It's no fun running aground in any boat, but size does matter. A smaller boat, with less mass, will hit with far less impact. When you're in a sailing vessel that's 110 feet long, with a tall wooden mast with yardarms attached to it, you're going to feel it, and it's not going to be fun.

When the ship landed, we felt the shudder run through the entire boat. We were lying on the shoal, leaning over about 35 to 40 degrees, and every wave picked us up slightly again, and dropped us again. Each time, the mast, yardarms, and rigging would groan and swing wildly. It seemed like forever, but within a minute the Coast Guard boat managed to back up to us, toss us a towing hawser with plenty of slack, and pull us back to the center of the channel. We secured the hawser to the anchoring and towing stanchion at the bow and signaled the Coast Guard that we were secure. They quickly pulled forward, taking the slack out of the hawser, and hit the power. Every time the waves picked up the Providence, it moved a bit forward, and by the third or fourth wave, we could see the mast begin to move back to upright as the ship was slowly pulled off the sandy shoal and back into the channel. By the fifth swell, we'd managed to clear the shoal, and the Coast Guard radioed that they'd tow us the rest of the way into calmer waters.

The first thought I had when we hit the shoal was concern for the strength of the hull. Although the ship was a replica of a Revolutionary War fighting frigate, the builders had wisely stayed away from building a wooden hull and had instead opted for a very heavy molded fiberglass hull, which, as we learned, had been a very wise decision, one which had prevented the grounding from becoming disastrous. Once we were safely in port and had gone over the interior of the hull looking for cracks and leaks and finding none, we hit our bunks well past midnight, exhausted, tired, and strangely exhilarated. The crew talked about the grounding a lot over the following days, and discovered that once the danger had passed, it was replaced by a realization that we'd survived a dangerous experience and were the better for it. We all felt like seasoned, veteran tall ship sailors after that experience. Plus, we all found ourselves with a real adventure story to tell, including our paying passengers, who were left awfully wide-eyed by the whole experience.

After the grounding along the Outer Banks, we had just one more stop in Newport News, and then it was on to the ship's home port at Fort

Adams in Narragansett Bay. After that long, eventful journey up the coast, it was nice to know the end was in sight. A large party was held onboard the day after our return, and after a few days partying in Newport, I headed over to visit my sister in Storrs, Connecticut for a few days, and then I hopped a bus back to Key West, unsure of what I'd do next.

THREE

SMUGGLING 101

Upon arriving home, I took a few days to relax and then started looking for a job. I wasn't in a rush, and I wasn't looking forward to a "regular" job working 9 to 5 after such a great adventure. I felt I'd earned the right to do something more exciting and in line with my new experience, but nothing was forthcoming. After a few weeks of searching, I found a job as a night watchman at Oceanside Marina, a large marina on the Atlantic side of Stock Island. It wasn't much of a job, but I had the night shift, so I spent my nights from 11 P.M. to 7 A.M. sitting in a guard shack and monitoring the comings and goings of residents and guests, as well as walking the docks once or twice a night. It wasn't a stressful job, and I had no supervision, so I used the quiet hours to write. Over the months that followed, I began writing in notebooks and wasn't too picky about what I wrote. I filled several notebooks with rambling, stream-of-consciousness writing about anything and everything that drifted through my mind while I watched the hours tick away until morning. About five years earlier, while summering in Pennsylvania at my parents' house, I'd taken off and hitchhiked across the United States and up through Canada to visit Alaska. It was a trip that blew my young mind, and I still think about it today. I mostly wrote about the events of the trip, from day one until the day I returned to Pennsylvania about two months later. I still have those notebooks to this day.

After a few months of working the security guard job, I found a note on my desk when I arrived at work one day, with a phone number to call. It was Mark, saying he wanted to talk to me about a business opportunity. He asked me how soon I could get up to Miami, and I immediately made plans to go up on my day off. I correctly guessed what sort of opportunity was being offered, and after he picked me up at the bus stop in Coconut Grove, just south of downtown Miami, he drove me to a nice neighborhood filled with new condominiums and flashy apartment complexes. It was there that I first met Garry, a man in his fifties with salt-and-pepper hair and a bit of a rooster. I learned he was a married man with a wife and several kids but lived separately from them with his twenty-five-year-old girlfriend Sarah. He also had another girlfriend on the West Coast, in Los Angeles, whom he stayed with when in LA. Somehow, they all made it work and were good friends, although Sarah wasn't close to Garry's other girlfriend, Bebe, the young Los Angeles woman of Mexican-Japanese descent who was fluent in Spanish.

Garry and I chatted for about an hour, and I could tell he was assessing me and sizing me up. Apparently, I'd come highly recommended by Mark, and Garry was just making sure Mark wasn't exaggerating about my sailing skills. After I passed that test, Garry got right to the point and asked me if I'd be interested in doing a run to Mexico to pick up a shipment of weed from a contact in Alvarado, Mexico, a little town way off the tourist routes, and smack in the middle of cartel country. The plan was to set sail for Cozumel, a tourist area, with me, Mark, another friend of theirs, and Bebe. Bebe would be our interpreter if needed but would only sail down with us and return on a plane with Garry.

After arriving in Cozumel and spending a few days partying and diving, we'd weigh anchor, head north and then east into the Bay of Campeche, meet up with our contacts in the shipping port of Veracruz, and then sail down the coast to our pickup point near the small town of Alvarado, which sat just inland on a huge lagoon named Laguna de Alvarado, fed by the Papaloapan River. It was there we'd load our weed and sail straight back to the Florida Keys in one long haul.

I didn't have to think about what my answer would be. I'd dreamed of this moment and waited for years for the opportunity. I immediately said yes and suddenly found myself planning my first smuggling trip. Our boat, a 52-foot Morgan ketch, had been rented out by Garry, and after I'd quit my job at the marina, I quickly returned to Miami to get the boat down to the Keys so we could stock up for the trip and go over any last-minute plans. We motored down the Intracoastal Waterway to Key Largo and then left the waterway and set sail for Key West, arriving at Oceanside Marina (the place I'd been working), where we planned the trip in more detail.

I could already see one problem brewing, and I hoped it would sort itself out quickly before it became a serious problem. Garry hadn't officially appointed me captain, and on the trip down to Key West, the boat was run by committee, which is never a good idea and cannot work in an emergency where things had to be done quickly and right. Since Mark had helped organize the trip, he tried taking control but really didn't know enough about boats to know what he was doing. His other friend Jerry, a Vietnam vet who still seemed to have some issues with PTSD, was pretty laid back and didn't get in the way, but I could see a battle of wills taking place between Mark and Bebe, who was going to sail with us to keep an eye on Garry's interests. Neither knew anything about sailing, but both wanted to be in charge. Since I was the one who knew how to sail, I just gave the orders when we were underway, but once we docked, I'd just back off and let them fight it out. I decided I'd wait patiently and if the shit hit the fan while we were at sea, I'd be the guy they turned to.

The trip took another fun turn a few days before our departure. We took the Morgan out for a few shakedown sails and cruised about the island and into the harbor a few times, once during sunset. As we slowly drifted back out of the harbor with a light wind and a changing tide, we sailed past the Pier House down next to Mallory Square. We were drifting slowly, as the wind was light and the tide was just about slack. As we passed the Pier House, I noticed a beautiful young woman on the deck, waving at us. I waved back and raised my drink in a toast as we sailed past, making eye contact the entire time. As we began to pass the dock at Mallory Square, where the crowds were lined up for the sunset, she shouted, "Take me with you!"

I laughed and shouted back, "I'd love to! Are you staying there?" I was referring to the Pier House.

"Yes," she shouted. "Come see me!"

I tried to shout my name and get hers, but we were too far away, and the noise from the pier drowned her out. I could have turned about and made another pass but decided to just enjoy the fun moment for what it was.

But my curiosity got the best of me, and the next day I took a trip down to the Pier House on the outside chance I'd run into her. I didn't know her name and didn't even know if she'd be around. If she was a tourist, she was probably out doing something fun. I couldn't ask for her at the desk since I had no name, but I decided to hang out by the beach bar for a bit. I'd no sooner taken a seat when I saw her down by the water on a chaise lounge, tanning and enjoying a cocktail. I had a decision to make. I wasn't an outgoing type when it came to approaching women, but since she'd been the one shouting at me, I assumed there was some interest. I downed my drink, grabbed another, and headed over to her chair.

She saw me coming, sat up, and smiled.

"Hey! You came back, sailor!"

Up close, she was even prettier than I'd noticed the night before. She had long brown hair, bleached from the sun, and green eyes with gray flecks, and her smile was infectious and pure. I detected no guile, just a beautiful woman with a fun and adventurous soul.

"I'm Kelly. How are you?"

"I'm Tiana. I'm fine. I'm glad you came back." She motioned to a chaise lounge near hers, and I pulled it over and sat down.

The attraction was mutual and instantaneous. She was exciting, smart, and quickly let me know that she had done a lot of sailing. We talked boats for a bit, the places we'd been and what we hoped to do. She listened while I rambled on about my childhood dreams coming true, and when I was done, she sat up and leaned in close.

"So, Kelly. What are you guys up to? Where are you going? Is that your boat?"

"No, it's a charter. I'm a freelance skipper, and we're running it down to Cozumel for a client. Not sure how long we'll be there, but hopefully for a week or two."

Her face lit up. "Cozumel! What a great spot! I go there often. It's more laid back and not quite as commercial as Cancun. Cheaper, too. I have some friends down there right now."

"Are they vacationing, or there for a while?"

"Oh, they rent a bungalow out on the windward side of the island. They'll be there for a few months. They're not like regular tourists. They like to live in a place for months rather than visit for a few weeks." She paused and laughed. "They have money, clearly!"

"Well, I'm not sure when we'll be leaving, but definitely within a few days. We go out every day for fun, so if you're free tomorrow and would like to join us, you're more than welcome."

"I'd love that! How long are you in the area?"

"Well, actually, I live here and have a small apartment up on Margaret Street. But I'm pretty sure we'll be taking off within the next few days, so if you'd like to join us tomorrow, I'll come get you."

"I'd love that! And I have a question for you. Feel free to say no if I'm being too forward."

I couldn't imagine anything she'd say that I'd think was too forward, but she surprised me by asking if she could join us on the trip to Cozumel. I'd just met her, and she knew nothing about me, and I knew nothing about her other than the fact that she was gorgeous and I had liked her immediately. I think she probably knew what we were up to when she raised an eyebrow and asked me how much weed the boat might carry. I laughed and immediately started wondering if I was talking to a narc. She sensed my surprise and change in tone and laughed it off by saying exactly what I was thinking.

"No, I'm not a narc! Just a joke!"

We chatted and drank on the beach for a few more hours. I found her amazing. She'd grown up in the northeast and had sailed Long Island Sound and Narragansett Bay as a child, suggesting she'd come from a fairly well-to-do family. She loved sailing, and she'd been on charters in the Virgin Islands on several occasions. I told her I'd have to check with my employer, and I had no idea what Garry would say. I knew he enjoyed being around younger women, so I thought it was worth a try.

In those days, a flight from Cozumel to Miami was about $150 US, and I knew lots of people in the Keys who regularly jumped on the short flight for quick vacations there, so it wasn't a stretch to think that Tiana would want to hitch a fun ride down to Cozumel on a sailboat, have some fun sailing for a few days, and then catch a cheap flight back to the States. I asked Garry that evening if Tiana could join us and was surprised when he quickly said it was okay without even meeting her. He then explained that a sailboat arriving in Cozumel with a bunch of young men and women wouldn't arouse any suspicion, whereas a sailboat with three guys on it would instantly attract attention with the Federales, honest or otherwise.

And just like that, within a matter of two weeks, I went from security guard at a marina to being the *de facto* skipper of a smuggling vessel headed for the Bay of Campeche to pick up several tons of Mexican weed, in the company of a gorgeous young woman I'd just met who happened to love sailing as much as me. The years of dreaming about it were over. I was officially a Key West pirate, about to set sail on my first trip, with a lovely woman by my side. I was excited about it and found myself walking around with a newfound swagger.

I'll take a moment here to explain my views on what I was about to do. At the time, I honestly never really thought about the fact that I was willfully getting ready to commit several felonies. I didn't think of myself as a criminal, and I didn't really think of smuggling as a serious crime, although I certainly knew it was against the law. I never thought about smuggling in a negative way, but more as an exciting, heart-stopping adventure on the high seas. What could be more exciting than sailing the Caribbean, drinking rum and smoking fine weed in tropical ports, loading your sailboat with high-quality marijuana, and sneaking it back into the States past the Coast Guard and DEA? Any way I looked at it, it just seemed like a very grand adventure, and I simply didn't see myself as a criminal. I was just a twenty-something adrenaline junkie, out to have a blast doing things I loved and making some cash in the process. Looking back from my current perspective, I'm still shocked at how naïve I was about everything, but I wasn't worried about anything at the time. While working, I was always vigilant about law enforcement, but also took huge risks just for excitement, which I'll get into a bit later in this tale.

At last, we set sail for Cozumel, and it was one of the best days of my life. I don't ever recall feeling so purely high on life and thinking I had the entire world at my feet. As we sailed past the Marquesas Keys toward the Dry Tortugas, the sails drawing smartly, the weather beautiful, sitting at the wheel of a gorgeous ketch with a beautiful, cool woman sitting beside me,

I just smiled and smiled and smiled, like a baby without a bad thought in its head.

Everything felt perfect, and I never wanted that moment to end. We watched a beautiful sunset off our bow and prepared for our first night on the open sea. Tiana and I took the first watch, while everyone else went below to sleep. I set the boat on autopilot, and as the wind was gentle and steady, I didn't worry much about a sudden shift causing any problems with the sails. We were right on the northern edge of the Gulfstream and would skirt the outside of the strong current until we eventually would have to sail right into it to get to Cozumel. But that wasn't on my mind that evening. Tiana and I were in the cockpit alone for most of the night, and it was one of the most romantic evenings I'd ever experienced. It was magical, sailing out of American waters into the open sea, sails full, a bit high from cocktails and weed, talking about anything, laughing at everything, her warm, tanned skin against mine, and music drifting softly out of the cockpit speakers, stars dancing overhead, the water lapping gently against the hull, bioluminescence trailing off the rudder like the trail of a comet as we sailed through the night.

FOUR

MEXICO

The cruise to Cozumel took about four days, and the first two were completely uneventful. On the third day we encountered a squall that came up suddenly, and we were hit hard, forcing us to quickly furl the sails and turn on the motor to ride more smoothly in the choppy seas, caused by strong winds blowing opposite a strong current. The squall blew through, followed by a proper storm that kicked up the waves even more. Adding to our problem was the fact that our LORAN system was on the fritz—or just appeared to be. Although I'd used them for navigation on many occasions, I didn't own one and didn't know enough about them to know exactly what was wrong with it. What was actually happening was that we were out of the range of one signal station, and I had no idea how to find a new one. I knew how to find my location on one, but I had no idea how to reset it or perform any troubleshooting. Although I'd used LORAN for navigating before, it had always been in a smaller area where there had never been a need to locate a new signal from a different LORAN station. With only one signal station to track, I didn't know precisely where we were. It was the equivalent of knowing what latitude you were sailing but not the longitude. I knew we were far enough at sea to avoid hitting anything, and I'd brought my sextant with me, so I planned to take a sun sight the next day to get a better idea of where we were in relation to the Yucatan peninsula.

It was at this point that I finally solidified my position as skipper. Mark and Jerry knew nothing about navigation. I could tell that Bebe had taken my side once I found our position with the sextant the following day, plotted a new course, and got us safely to the Mexican coast by nightfall. From that point, we stayed offshore in international waters, turned on the motor to help fight the strong Gulfstream current, and using navigational lights visible on shore, I guided the boat throughout the night, dropping anchor in Cozumel the following morning. Garry already had a nice hotel booked for us, at the El Presidente down the coast from town, and after clearing customs, we moved the boat south and anchored just offshore of the hotel.

Tiana got off and said her goodbyes. She didn't make a big deal of it . . . just a big smile, a thanks for a wonderful time, and she was gone in a cab. I think she was waiting for me to ask for her contact information, but I dropped the ball. She was a mirror image of me, a female version, living every moment to the fullest, and not thinking about the future. I thought that would be the last time I ever saw her, and I knew I would always remember her fondly.

Bebe moved ashore to Garry's hotel room, and Mark, Jerry, and I remained on the boat. Over a fine dinner that night, Garry announced to us all that I was now officially the captain, and everyone would take orders from me while at sea. No discussion, no more committee work. I looked over at Bebe, who smiled and nodded at me, letting me know that she had spoken to Garry and convinced him to give me full control. She might have just been Garry's girlfriend, but she was also keeping an eye on his operation, and I was grateful to her for convincing Garry that I was the best bet to get the boat to its destinations and home safely with our cargo. I was officially Captain Kelly, smuggling boat captain.

We spent a few days in Cozumel, getting the boat restocked with food and water, and learning a lot more about how to fully operate the boat's LORAN. A local charter captain spent an hour with me, teaching me everything he knew about the electronic navigation systems on the boat, and by the end of the afternoon, I was confident in my skills with electronics, primarily because I was confident in my skills with a sextant, should the electronics fail. It was decided that Bebe would stay on the boat for the next leg of the trip when we'd sail from Cozumel, up and around the Yucatan peninsula, and down to Veracruz, where she'd officially remove herself from the crew list and stay with Garry from that point on.

The sail from Cozumel to Veracruz was uneventful, just day after day of blissful sailing in near-perfect weather. We only ran the engine a few hours a day to keep the battery charged and occasionally ran the generator so that we could turn on the air conditioning in the cabin and cool off in the heat of the day. The Morgan was a mid-level luxury sailboat with several waterproof speakers in the cockpit, so we always had music playing. On a few occasions, we had no wind, so we'd fire up the engine and motor until the wind picked back up again. We drank a lot of beer, smoked a lot of weed, ate well, and generally enjoyed life under sail on the open ocean. It was almost everything I'd dreamed of. In my reveries, I was alone with the woman of my dreams, just the two of us, and no other crew. It made me think of Tiana and how perfect she seemed in every way. But this gang would have to do. If the trip went as planned, I'd be buying my own sailboat and starting a new life as a live-aboard in the Keys, free to go where I wanted, whenever I wanted.

We didn't see any other sailboats in the Bay of Campeche, but we encountered lots of commercial freighters, coming at us from every angle. Some passed very close to us, and several times we found ourselves on intersecting courses and had to move out of the way or get run down. We noticed many freighters with Russian names on them, as well as ships from ports all over the world, and assumed that Veracruz must be a major international shipping port. Upon arriving, while checking in with the local customs office, we learned that Veracruz did business with over 150 countries on all the major continents, a fact the locals were very proud to tell us.

It was immediately obvious that Veracruz wasn't a tourist town. Everything looked run-down and dirty along the docks, and it was all business. There was a distinct lack of the usual things we'd grown used to in tourist destinations, like the presence of cruise ships, and bars and restaurants catering to gringos. It wasn't until we made our way into the center of the city that things brightened up, and we shopped for fresh food, as we hadn't had anything fresh in days, and we were tired of canned and freeze-dried items. We decided to get some local steaks but nearly passed when we visited an open market and saw a side of beef hanging in the sun, with flies covering the outside. We were assured by a local that the meat would be excellent, and that he'd trim off the first half inch of the exposed surface. We watched several other locals purchase steaks, and they also assured us there was no problem, so we purchased several large steaks, cut right from the hot, sunbaked hind quarter. We were doubtful, but when we grilled it up later that evening, we were very surprised at how good it tasted. I certainly wouldn't have guessed it earlier, though. After a week on the boat, we were ready for a real shower and a real bed, and Garry didn't disappoint us. He'd booked hotel rooms at a small resort down the coast, away from the city, so we sailed down the coast and once again anchored in front of the hotel where we would be staying.

As this wasn't a tourist area, nor a prime sailing destination, we immediately caused a big commotion, as people rarely saw a yacht in this area. We quickly realized that we needed some sort of cover story, so we devised an elaborate story about Garry being a real estate developer from Texas who was looking to build a resort in the area, and we were his crew. Within hours, a reporter from the local newspaper showed up and wanted to do a story about us. We didn't want to decline and arouse any suspicion, so Garry agreed to sit for the story. The reporter, a woman named Dolly, arrived with a photographer and sat us all down for an interview. Fortunately, she didn't speak English, so most of the story was told to her through Bebe, who acted as an interpreter, and any holes in our story were glossed over as things lost in translation. The reporter never showed any signs of being suspicious of our true intentions, the story ran in the next day's paper, with photographs, and I still have a copy of the article to this day, tucked away in a scrapbook somewhere.

After a few days of rest and relaxation at the small resort, we continued down the coast to Alvarado. There was a large suspension bridge over the entrance to the lagoon, and we weren't certain our mast would clear it, so we anchored just downstream. During high tide, the ocean created a very strong current that pushed seawater upstream into the lagoon, and when the tide dropped, the powerful water flow reversed itself, the water in the lagoon, fed by a river, rushed back out the opposite direction. It was a very strong tidal flow, and we constantly worried about our anchor not holding during the strongest points in the tidal shift. We made sure we had someone on the boat during that time, just in case the anchor pulled. Because the lagoon was fed by a river, we'd often see all sorts of debris heading out with the tide, even trees on occasion.

When high tide approached, the river looked like seawater as it pushed inland, and at low tide, it reversed and turned back into a muddy river as the lagoon emptied. Alvarado sat just on the other side of the bridge, so if we went ashore for any reason, we took our inflatable skiff with an outboard motor up to the harbor.

Upon arrival, Garry met up with our local Mexican cartel contact, a young man named Oscar. It became clear that Oscar was a no-nonsense player and always packed a gun in his waistband. He didn't speak much English, and our Spanish was rudimentary and limited to "Una más cerveza, por favor," and a few other phrases. We decided it was important to know how to order a beer and recognize swear words, and we built our vocabulary from that base.

Oscar was in charge of getting the load from the hills out to the boat and seemed like a competent guy for his age. He also seemed to enjoy our company and smiled at us a lot. Because of the communication barrier, we didn't speak much, but he made it clear that he'd like to take us ashore one night and show us around town, an invitation I quickly accepted, along with Mark and Jerry. Bebe and Garry would stay on the boat. We met Oscar at the dock where we left our skiff under the protection of some kids, who were paid by Oscar. We were assured that nobody would touch it once they knew that it was under the protection of a cartel member. We also felt that we were safe around town while in his company, but we also wondered if he might have any enemies out to get him. It was an exciting evening, to put it simply. Everyone seemed to know exactly who he was, and we got into all the clubs and were given great service. Oscar clearly enjoyed being host to the Americanos, although at one club he was challenged by the doorman for carrying a pistol. There was a brief stare down, and the doorman didn't back down. Oscar paused for a bit, then slapped the guy's arm in a friendly manner before turning to us and nodding to move away. We learned that the club belonged to a "competidor," a rival, according to Oscar, which is why he was challenged. We assumed that the doorman didn't want an armed cartel member in the club. The word competidor in Spanish sounded almost identical to the English counterpart, and we recognized instantly what Oscar was telling us, so we agreed to move on to avoid any trouble.

One of the highlights of the night was standing on a brightly lit street eating tiny, bite-sized street tacos, made with crispy fried pork, some fresh pico, and smothered with a scalding green chile sauce. They came in orders of five, and I quickly went through two orders. We were slightly drunk and quite high, and the food was incredible. If I recall, most food tasted incredible when you were drunk and high. I remember quickly devouring those tacos, enjoying every bite, filling my lungs with the night air, and my head with the sounds of nighttime street life in a coastal Mexican town that never saw tourists. I'd been in many tourist vacation spots in my life, but this was the first time I was completely off the beaten path, in a place that never saw any gringos. The whole experience was made more interesting by the fact that our host was an armed Mexican cartel member. It added an element of danger and risk to the street taco experience, standing around enjoying the mouthfuls of savory, seasoned pork, smothered in green sauce, sprinkled with the vague threat of a violent death in the jungle, something we wouldn't likely experience at a safe tourist destination, or disco dancing at Carlos & Charlie's in Cozumel.

We returned to the boat that night and learned that the following evening would be our last in Alvarado. Just after dusk the next day, we'd sail offshore, anchor, and wait for the boats to arrive with our shipment. After breakfast, we took Garry and Bebe ashore, said our goodbyes, and returned to the boat. We spent the day relaxing, smoking weed, working on our tans, and making sure the sailboat was ready for the return trip to the Keys. The return trip would cover over 1,000 nautical miles, and we'd be sailing with thousands of pounds of Mexican marijuana tucked away in the berths below. We'd be averaging anywhere from 120 to 160 miles a day, depending on wind and weather, so we were looking at well over a week at sea, with no help on the way if anything went bad for us. Any problems that needed fixing would have to be solved by me and the crew. Our immediate concern was to be free of Mexican waters as quickly as possible and hope that word of our shipment hadn't leaked to any rival cartel members who might pull a "freelancer" move, and have the cojones to hijack our shipment, steal it and our boat, and kill us in the process.

It was a valid concern that we talked about, and all we had on the boat for defensive weapons was an old single-shot shotgun and a box of shells, and a flare gun with 10 flares. Hardly enough to mount a defense if swarmed by cartel members with AK-47s. To compound matters, Jerry was a Vietnam veteran who had seen a lot of combat and was particularly paranoid about being attacked. We decided to let him stay below and stack the bales when they arrived, just to make him feel a bit safer, as he was convinced that our own Mexican crew was out to burn us. I was certain that Oscar would make sure we weren't in any danger, but double-crosses weren't unheard of in those days, so we decided to remain vigilant during the loading.

Just after sunset, we pulled anchor in the inlet and motored out with the falling tide. It was a full moon, which worried us because the hull of the sailboat was white and could be seen for a long distance. We knew that we'd be very visible anchored offshore, even if we anchored beyond the sandy alluvial fan at the mouth of the inlet. The sandy bottom quickly dropped off about half a mile from shore, and as we didn't know the composition of the bottom, we decided to anchor about half a mile offshore. We would be sitting ducks, but we had no options. We crossed our fingers and hoped that Oscar was exactly the guy we thought he was.

This being my first pickup and loading operation as a smuggler, I willed myself to calm down, but my heart was racing. Many different scenarios with many different outcomes raced through my mind, and I started developing some of Jerry's paranoia about the cartel's intentions. Let's face it—we were defenseless, and we were on a boat worth a lot of money, and from what I knew, we'd already paid for the shipment. If someone in the Mexican side of the operation decided to screw us over, there was nothing we'd be able to do but put up a brief fight. I knew I wouldn't feel comfortable until we were loaded and fifty miles offshore.

As we sat at anchor, I relaxed on the deck and drank a beer and smoked a joint to calm my nerves. The coast of Mexico was beautiful in the moonlight, and the sailboat rose and fell gently with the swells. Lights twinkled along the shore, and the breeze, moving offshore from the land, smelled like a forest after a rain. I finally got myself calmed down a bit, and within minutes heard outboard engines approaching us. I couldn't see the boats, but by the sound I could tell that there were at least two. I couldn't see anything too clearly until they were within 100 yards and noticed that the hulls of the skiffs were painted black, and the men in the boats were all dressed in dark clothes. Even in the moonlight they were hard to see from any distance, but they certainly had no problem finding us.

As the boats pulled up alongside us, one of the men threw me a bow line, which I tied off on a cleat near the mast on our boat, and then pulled them close to us with a stern line. The first boat rested comfortably against the large rubber fenders I'd hung over the side, and within seconds, the first bales started coming over the side onto the deck. Nobody from the skiff tried to board us, which was a relief, but that meant that I would have to handle every bale as it came off the skiff, pass it to Mark in the cockpit, who'd then hand it to Jerry below deck, where he'd have to quickly stack it and get ready for the next one. After about a minute of this, I realized that Jerry wouldn't be able to stack fast enough, so I shouted to him and told him to just toss everything forward, and we'd do a proper packing job later, once we were underway. This adjustment solved the flow issue, and within twenty minutes, both skiffs had unloaded and were turning back toward shore.

During the transfer, not a word was exchanged between me and any of the men on the boat. I was expecting Oscar to be there, but I never saw him. He'd apparently insulated himself from grunt work and other activities that might expose him to arrest, which suggested he was a mid-level local manager, someone who let others take the jobs with the highest risk of contact with the Federal Ministerial Police, the group most often working to combat organized crime in Mexico. After the last bale came aboard, the man who'd been passing bales to me quickly untied from our boat, nodded toward me, gave me a small wave of the hand, and within seconds disappeared back into the night.

As soon as they untied, I started up the motor, had Mark pull anchor, and I turned toward the sea and quickly had the boat motoring away from shore at around seven knots. I had one goal at that moment, and it was to put as much distance between us and the Mexican coast as I possibly could. I didn't turn on any running lights, and the charts showed nothing but deep water ahead, so we motored straight away from shore for over two hours before deciding to shut down the engine and raise the sails. During that time, Mark and Jerry organized the load below, stowing most of the weed amidships for balance. It was important not to get too much weight forward, because if we ran into heavy seas, we did not want to be bow-heavy and risk swamping the decks as we rose and fell with the swells. Had we been making this trip in coastal waters, we might have loaded the boat differently, but the decision to optimize the weight distribution would play a crucial role in our safety in the coming days.

FIVE

HOMEWARD BOUND

Several hours after loading, we were in international waters and ready for what we hoped would be a relaxing sail back to American waters and home. Unfortunately, that wouldn't be true. We made it through the night without incident, but within an hour after sunrise, the winds stopped, and we found ourselves sitting on a flat, glassy ocean with barely a ripple. The sails hung limp, and we were dead in the water. We wanted to conserve as much diesel fuel as possible, as the sailboat only had a motoring range of a few hundred miles, and we didn't want to take any chances of running out on the return trip. While sailing to Veracruz the previous week, we'd run the generator more than we should have to keep the air conditioning running below decks. It was very hot in the Bay of Campeche, and Mark had grown accustomed to having the air conditioning on for extended periods when he was off watch and sleeping below. As a result of running the air conditioning so often, we'd run low on our fuel supply, and while anchored in the inlet below Alvarado, we'd run the diesel tank dry and had to fill up a jerry can from a local marina to get it started up again so that we could get to a dock and refuel.

The fuel tank was now full, but we also knew we didn't have an infinite supply, so I insisted that we stop running the air conditioner for the remainder of the trip. From that point on, all our fuel was for the engine only, and Mark would just have to open some windows to stay comfortable. What I didn't realize was that the simple act of running the tank dry had created a big problem that hadn't yet reared its head but would do so very soon.

So, there we sat. A 52-foot sailboat in the southern Gulf of Mexico, stuffed to the gills with bales of marijuana, dead in the water and surrounded by shipping lanes and freighters that would not be changing their course for us, should we drift into their path. We knew we would have to use the motor, but this early in the trip, I was cautious about using it too often and running out of fuel. Not only would we lose our ability to get out of danger's way if the wind quit, but we'd also lose the generator and the ability to keep our batteries charged up. Without batteries, we'd have no LORAN, and I'd have to use a sextant to navigate us back to US waters.

I planned to avoid drawing suspicion by sailing high into the Gulf of Mexico toward the west coast of Florida and then sailing on a slightly southeast course back to the Keys. I knew that the Coast Guard and the DEA airplanes focused most of their efforts on the Straits of Florida, with most of the smuggling boat traffic coming up through the Yucatan Channel, turning the corner near Cuba, and heading northeast in the Straits of Florida. My course had us completely avoiding this area and coming back to the Keys from a course tracking from the northwest. I knew that boat traffic in the Straits was closely monitored, and suspicious boats tracked as they came through the Yucatan Channel, so we'd be safe, and probably identified on radar as a fishing trawler or shrimping boat, as there'd be many in the area we'd have to sail through as we approached US waters. I knew it was a good plan, even though it involved being at sea an extra day or two.

I made the decision to run the motor a bit and run slowly at about 4 knots to avoid heavy fuel consumption. The breeze was almost non-existent, and even when it was blowing, it barely filled the sails. With the inconsistent wind and having to motor, we quickly fell behind schedule and only traveled about 70 nautical miles in a twenty-four-hour period. All we could do was hope for a breeze and conserve our fuel as much as possible.

On the third evening, we had a very slight breeze that allowed us to maintain our course at a pace of around two or three knots per hour. It wasn't fast, and it wasn't getting us back on schedule, but it kept us moving just fast enough to be able to control the boat and have responsive steering. I was off watch that evening, sleeping quietly below, when I woke suddenly.

I could always sense when a freighter was near, as it created almost imperceptible sounds and vibrations against the hull, and if you had your head on a pillow, and knew what to listen for, you could tell you were near a ship. Most people I sailed with never experienced it, but I had developed a sixth sense about it, and whenever I was resting below deck and felt it, I quickly went above to check out the situation. I woke suddenly and sensed that a ship was close to us, and I immediately sensed that it was far closer than I wanted to be. I stuck my head out the hatch and was shocked to see a freighter bearing down on us, less than a quarter mile away. Jerry was at the helm, wide awake, but seemingly oblivious to the oncoming ship, and he hadn't corrected the course to avoid it. I looked at the ship and shouted at him. He looked startled and puzzled, like I was making a fuss about nothing.

It was moving fast. Jerry didn't seem to grasp the danger, which angered me. Ocean freighters have an average cruising speed of over 20 knots, but because of their size, they don't appear to be moving very quickly. This one was bearing down on us at a high rate of speed, and as it grew larger in a matter of thirty seconds, he suddenly realized the danger he'd put us in. I started up the motor as quickly as possible, luffed the sails, and steered the boat away from the path of the freighter. Had I not come topside when I did, I'm certain we would have been struck by the ship. Even with my quick response, the freighter's wake tossed us and rocked the boat wildly, waking Mark, who'd been still sleeping below. The ship took forever to pass us, and we had to crane our necks up to see the top of the ship's railing. It passed so close that I could see crew members above us on the pilot house deck, pointing at us as they passed. They had to have seen us on their radar, but couldn't, or wouldn't, change course for us. If the ship had struck us, we'd have been smashed. I was shaking and angry at Jerry, who still didn't seem to grasp the full extent of the danger he'd exposed us to by not paying attention to his surroundings. I just stood there and kept looking at him, shaking my head. What the hell had he been thinking?

The experience left me a bit rattled, and I realized I'd have to pay closer attention, whether I was on watch or not. I'd calmed down by morning but vowed to be more vigilant of lapses in judgment from the crew. We couldn't afford an accident of that nature on this trip.

Mark was also upset by the near miss and took it out on Jerry during his daytime watch. As I'd noted earlier, the yacht had waterproof speakers in the cockpit, and we got to choose what music we listened to if we were on watch. Mark had found a soundtrack to the movie "The Sound of Music" in the boat's cassette tape collection, so he locked the hatch with him and me below and put in the cassette on loop. For the remainder of the watch, Jerry was locked out of the boat, trapped in the cockpit, forced to listen to The Sound of Music soundtrack over and over for hours. I could have ended it, but I was still a bit pissed at Jerry, so I went along with it and had a good laugh, especially when Mark and I began singing along, serenading Jerry through the hatch. Jerry wasn't pleased but said nothing when his watch ended. He told me later that he would never be able to hear a single song from that soundtrack without thinking about that experience.

Things seemed to fall apart after the near miss. The weather was becoming increasingly mild, and we were barely making 3 knots for long stretches of time. We simply didn't have the food and supplies for more than about ten days at sea, and I was worried we'd run out of fuel if we began running under power twenty-four hours a day. Within a day, my worst worries would come true. To that point, we'd avoided any bad weather. In fact, the weather had been too mild, and we weren't making headway, and we lacked the fuel to run under power back to the Keys. Something would have to give.

By evening, I could see storm clouds brewing ahead of us. This was 1981, and we weren't equipped with a long-range radio that could alert us to bad weather coming our way. We simply dealt with whatever came our way and made the best of it. The storm moving toward us wasn't coming quickly, but I knew we'd run into it around nightfall. The one positive thing that happened was an increase in wind, and after several days at sea, we were about to experience the first good wind of our return trip to the States. Throughout the afternoon, we had a very brisk wind coming on to our starboard bow, and it made for some spirited sailing. It came from a perfect direction for us to run close-hauled on the same tack for the entire day. By late afternoon, it was strong enough to put a double reef in the mainsail and drop the mizzen completely, running with just the reefed main and jib. Although the boat was well equipped, my only complaint with its sailing capabilities was the fact that we didn't have several jibs, but instead a single retracting roller jib, something I always hated on sailboats. They were great in good weather, but not ideal for being at sea in stormy conditions. I wished we had a selection of jibs on the boat, like a well-equipped seagoing sailboat should have had. But we had to make do with what we had, so I partially rolled in the jib until it was a small triangle. Because it bulged in the center where it met the rolling headstay, it didn't form a clean aerodynamic shape and constantly snapped in and out. It was annoying, but worse, inefficient, and we were stuck with the setup.

We were still under sail when the storm hit us shortly after dark. We felt the breeze change abruptly, and the air instantly felt different. The temperature dropped five or ten degrees in a matter of a minute, and the wind almost stopped. I sensed we were about to get slammed by the storm, and we dropped the mainsail but kept up the jib to maintain control. I reduced its size even farther until it was just a small triangle of sail. It wouldn't catch a lot of wind (or so I thought) but would provide some stability as we headed into the storm.

Within seconds after furling and securing the mainsail, we were slammed by the storm, and the waves picked up drastically. The bow began to rise and fall with the large waves, and I realized that the tiny jib might help me stay pointed in the right direction, but it wasn't going to help us make headway. I'd considered turning around partially and running off the edge of the storm, but that tack would have taken us farther up into the Gulf of Mexico, and depending upon how long it lasted, many miles off course, miles that would have to be retraced in the right direction. I decided to turn on the engine and run at just enough power to go right into the storm, hoping that the waves wouldn't get too high, and the rising and falling of the bow would be bearable, and not put us into any danger.

Once we were under power, I put on a harness with a rope and clipped myself to the boat's lifeline, a heavy, plastic-coated wire that ran around the perimeter of the boat through stainless steel stanchions bolted to the deck, and which provided a measure of safety in fair weather. In heavy weather, it was ideal to wear harnesses on deck with lanyards and clip yourself to the lifeline with carabiners. This allowed crew to work the entire deck safely even in bad weather. Unfortunately, this boat was only outfitted with one harness, so I had everyone else go below and close the hatch. I stayed in the cockpit, motor running, and we began pounding into the waves.

This was the worst storm I'd been in at sea in my sailing experience. The waves were building up quickly, and the boat was rising and falling at steep angles as the oncoming waves picked up the bow and then dropped it violently back into the water with a slam. I quickly grew concerned that the mast and rigging would tear loose, as I could hear it groaning with every violent pitch of the boat. I finally found the right speed to match the waves and lessen the impact of the bow with each drop, yet we were still climbing waves that were 30 to 40 degrees off level, and it was uncomfortable, to put it mildly. Although we were motoring under power, I don't think we were making any headway but simply holding our position as the waves rolled under us. This went on through the night, and both Mark and Jerry stayed below. They couldn't sleep because of the violent motion of the boat, and I wondered how long the storm would last. After several hours, the waves became steady and the brunt of the stormfront had moved past us, but the wind was still strong, and the waves still very high.

And then the engine quit. Not all at once, but it began to sputter and miss. It couldn't have picked a worse time to go, and I screamed for someone to get on deck and help me get some sails up quickly before we turned sideways in the trough of a wave and got rolled. Mark popped through the hatch and helped me set a small jib so that I would still be able to steer, and once it was set, we put up an equally small patch of the reefed mainsail and finally gained better tracking. This created a new problem, however, as we could no longer head right into the waves, but now had to tack off at an angle. Not only were we now rising and falling at steep angles with each wave, but as the bow went over each wave, the boat would roll violently from left to right, and then back again as it started up the edge of each swell. During this time, the engine continued to sputter and then finally quit.

It was past midnight, and I was curious where we were, so I had Mark take a LORAN reading and find our position. After a few minutes, he stuck his head up through the hatch.

"We've gained about five miles since our last reading," he said. Our last reading was five hours ago. We'd barely moved in the storm, as I suspected.

"Shit. At least we're not off course!" I shouted.

"And we're about 10 miles north of our course," he added. It could have been a lot worse, I told myself.

"Can you guys look at the engine and see what's going on? I know we're not out of fuel. We've barely used any since topping off in Alvarado."

"Jerry's sick," said Mark. "He's not moving around."

"Seasick? Or something else?"

"Just seasick. I'll look at the engine."

"You don't know anything about diesel engines. Jerry does. Tell him we need him."

Mark went below and closed the hatch. After a few minutes, he opened it again. "Jerry's going to look at the engine. He found the manual, and he thinks we probably got some air in the line when we ran the tank dry earlier. He's going to bleed it and see what happens."

"Tell him if he wants this rocking and rolling motion to stop, we'll have to get the engine running." I hoped that alone would be enough motivation.

Mark closed the hatch and went below again. I sat down for the first time in hours and kept the ketch pointed into the wind. Even with minimal sail, we seemed to be making better time, but we were also heeling over under the strong winds. "But at least we're making up time," I thought. For the first time that evening, I took a moment and relaxed. The swells were consistent, the wind still strong, the waves still high, but even under those conditions, the chaos that we'd dealt with earlier was gone. We were in a storm, but things were now settled, and we weren't seeing anything new. We just had to ride out the storm and somehow figure out how to get the diesel running again. After about twenty minutes, I heard the generator start up and run quietly, so whatever was affecting the engine was not a problem with the generator, which was a good sign. Even in a worst-case scenario, we'd still be able to charge our batteries and have our electronics for navigation.

Mark stuck his head through the hatch. "Try the engine," he said.

I turned the key, and the motor started up.

Mark grinned at me. "Jerry said there was air in the line. He just bled the line a bit."

I smiled back and gave him a thumbs-up. Things had just improved a lot, but my optimism was short-lived.

I kept the motor running at idle, but engaged, as we were still running under sail, and the motor added another knot to our speed through the water. After about thirty minutes, I was comfortable running under sail, and things seemed to be settling down. We were still in a storm, but everything was under control, and we would most likely be back on our charted course by morning. Just when I was getting comfortable and returning to a sense of normal, the engine quit again. I kicked the side of the cockpit to get Mark's attention. His head quickly popped up through the hatch.

"What the hell?" I asked.

"He said it's probably air in the line again. He's going to bleed it again." He slid the hatch door shut. I sat down, frustrated.

Within ten minutes, Mark slid the hatch open again. "Try the engine," he said.

I hit the starter again, and the engine fired up. "Did he get it right this time?" I asked.

Mark shrugged. "Who knows?" he said. That's not what I wanted to hear.

Within twenty minutes, the engine quit again. Jerry bled the fuel line again. It ran for another twenty minutes and quit again. This scenario played out through the remainder of the night, over and over, and as day broke over the ocean, I told Mark to just shut it down. Whatever Jerry was doing wasn't solving the problem completely, but if we could get twenty minutes of running time out of every fix, at least we knew our limitations. We would use the engine when we needed it. I told Jerry to bleed it again, but we just wouldn't start it up. It would be for emergency only, and I wanted it ready at all times.

With that problem out of the way, it didn't surprise me at all that another one quickly appeared to replace it. Although we had the jib rolled down to a tiny patch throughout the storm, the pressures on the grommet at the clew of the jib, the section where the jib sheet (the rope that controlled the jib) attached to the jib, were very strong and had slowly torn at the sailcloth to the point where the grommet ripped completely out of the sail. One of the many reasons I disliked roller jibs was that unless you put a cover on them, the trailing edge of the jib was exposed to sunlight all the time, and the sailcloth could become brittle after years of exposure to the sun. Although the sailcloth was doubled up and thickest at the clew, it was also very brittle, and the constant pressure and fluttering during the storm had taken its toll.

The tear in the jib came without warning. One moment we were sailing on a clean tack, the jib taut, and suddenly I heard a loud crack, and the jib was snapping loose in the strong winds. The crack I heard was the heavy clew hitting the hull. I turned on the engine again to point us directly into the wind, and had Mark take some short ropes and secure the flapping jib to the headstay. Now all we had was the mainsail, so to keep moving, we also reefed our mizzen mast so we'd have a bit more sail surface in the wind. It wasn't as efficient as the main and jib, but it worked and kept us headed upwind. I could tell we weren't moving as quickly as before the break, but at least we were moving. We ran under reefed main and mizzen through the remainder of the night and into the morning, which brought clearer skies and a greatly diminished breeze that allow us to take the reefs out of the sail.

We now had two problems to deal with. We had a diesel engine that wouldn't run more than twenty minutes without quitting and requiring us to bleed the fuel lines again, and no working jib. I thought about our problem for a bit and decided to jury-rig the jib the best I could. Fortunately, we had a sail sewing kit on board, and while Mark took the helm for the morning watch, I sat on the deck working on the torn jib. I folded the torn tip over a good section of the jib and sewed it around with edges to hold it in place. I then took a knife and cut a new hole in the clew where we could attach the sheets, or jib lines, to trim the sail. It looked terrible and clumsy, but it worked. I didn't think it would take another storm, but I knew it was enough to get us home under sail.

With that problem out of the way, I could finally refocus on the last leg of the trip. By noon that day, I checked our position, and we were about two hundred miles due west of the Florida Everglades. Key West was southwest of our position, and we'd be approaching from the northwest, which wouldn't attract any attention as the area was filled with trawlers, mostly shrimping boats, and we'd just be one of many boats showing up on a radar. We didn't fear the Coast Guard here, as I knew they focused their efforts to catch smugglers by patrolling the Gulfstream and the Straits of Florida, almost two hundred miles south of us. By now, we were out of deep waters and over the continental shelf, and we began encountering trawlers everywhere.

Most fished at night, so during the day they sat at anchor while the crews slept. We spent that day sailing easily, as the waves had dropped, the bad weather had passed, and we were back to a comfortable pace toward home, none the worse for wear other than our ailing diesel and torn jib.

This was the early 1980s, and the type of communication equipment available now simply wasn't available to us then. There were ways to stay in touch with people on shore while at sea, but we decided the best thing was to run silent and touch base when we arrived back in the Keys. We had a CB radio but that only worked when close to shore and we'd made no plans to contact anyone until we set foot on land again. Our plan was simple. We'd just sail into a marina, get a slip, contact Garry and figure out how we'd unload. We knew the boat would smell like marijuana and hoped nobody in law enforcement got wind of it and tried to investigate.

We sailed down between the Dry Tortugas and the Marquesas Keys and turned east toward Key West. We were now inside the reef that protected the Keys from heavy seas, and the sailing was pleasant. As we approached Key West, I could see that Jerry was getting nervous and paranoid again.

"Are you okay?" I asked him.

He shrugged. "I don't know. How are we going to handle this?"

"We're just going to sail right into Oceanside Marina, get a berth, and figure it out from there."

"How do you know we can get a slip? Are we going to have to pull up to the dock by the dock master's office? There are people everywhere. What if someone boards us?"

I'd thought of that, and decided that as soon as possible, I'd radio ahead, reserve a berth out near the last dock away from the crowds, and then walk to the dock master to settle up. With the Marquesas behind us, I started picking up the channel and shoal markers to our left, and as we passed Boca Grande Key, the island of Key West rose on the horizon before us. It was a welcome sight, and it was nice to be almost home. We weren't going to be safe, and I wasn't going to feel comfortable, until we had the boat unloaded and I knew we were in the clear. We just had to get the boat unloaded, and I still had no idea what Garry had in mind. I got on the ship to shore radio, contacted Oceanside Marina, asked for a slip on the dock closest to open water, and finally started to relax just a bit.

Seeing Key West off the port bow as we sailed toward Stock Island was a welcome site, and we were all relieved to be back in American waters. The island always looked inviting from the ocean, with only a few tall buildings downtown, and a few high-rise buildings out near the airport. We waved at tourists out on the White Street pier, and soon the channel marker for Oceanside Marina came in view. We were almost home, and excited to be this close to the finish line.

Without checking in at the dock masters, we motored right up to our berth at the end of the dock farthest from the dock master's office. Nobody was there to meet us, which was fine with us. We pulled in and tied off, and I walked to the dock master's office. I knew the dock master, and I'm pretty sure he knew what I was up to, but he never let on. We chatted a bit, and I mentioned that we'd just returned from the Dry Tortugas. Several other men were sitting around the office, and I didn't know any of them, so I was taking no chances. Any one of them could have been DEA or plainclothes Florida Marine Patrol officers. The dock master was uncommonly cordial, which I suspected was his way of letting me know to be vigilant. I'd been in his office many times when it was crowded with locals who lived in the marina, and he was always talkative and friendly. His seriousness suggested he didn't know these guys, and I took note.

Once I had us squared away with the marina paperwork, I went to a payphone and called Garry, who was still in Miami. This surprised me, as I expected to have Sarah (the one he lived with, not Bebe) answer the telephone and give me a local number for him. I told him we'd arrived, and he told me he'd be down first thing in the morning. It was a quick conversation, and nothing other than our arrival was discussed. I went back and told the crew that Garry wasn't in town but would be there tomorrow. They were as surprised as me and started to grumble about the apparent lack of preparation for our arrival.

While I was standing on the dock, away from the boat for the first time in weeks, I could clearly smell the weed on our boat. As much as I hated to do it, I had Jerry and Mark close all the windows and hatches and turn on the air conditioning, as we were now docked and had access to shore power. We had to avoid having anyone smell our cargo before we had a chance to unload it, and that seemed like the only way. Mark didn't mind, as he loved air conditioning, but I preferred to have ports and hatches open and breathe fresh sea air every chance I had.

Garry arrived early the next morning, seeming overly cheerful, which struck me as odd. He was accompanied by a Colombian man who seemed a bit rough around the edges, and not very friendly. I pulled Garry aside and asked about his companion.

"Who's that? What's he doing here?"

"He's one of Luis's men." Luis was the name used by the Colombian backing Garry's trip.

"He doesn't look friendly."

"He's a hitter," said Garry. A hitter, among our group, was basically a killer for hire, the muscle behind the power. "He's just here to keep an eye on things."

That sure made me more comfortable. I'd be under the watchful eye of a man who killed people. Doesn't everyone want to work under those conditions?

"What's our plan?" I asked Garry.

"I'm working on it," he said.

I would like to say I was surprised that nothing had been planned, but at this point in the game, nothing surprised me anymore. Every step of this trip seemed unplanned, and I remember just sighing and sitting down. Mark and I finally came up with an idea that seemed workable, and we presented it to Garry.

We knew a local diesel mechanic who worked on fishing trawlers, someone who had extensive time with diesel engines. We knew him to be discreet and someone who wouldn't have any problem working on a boat sitting in a marina filled with marijuana, if he was properly compensated with both cash and product. We would have him gain permission to drive his work van out onto the dock and park beside the boat. We needed to have the fuel line bled properly to get the engine working as it should, so we had a legitimate excuse for calling him. We explained the situation, and he was fine with the arrangement. Once he was parked on the dock beside the boat, the man who'd shown up with Garry pulled another old van onto the dock and parked next to the mechanic. I decided to walk over to the dock master's office to see if we'd aroused any attention. I bought a beer in the cantina and walked into the dock master's hut. The usual gang of retirees sat around inside. I didn't see any strangers, which gave me a sense of relief.

"How's it going today?" asked Gabe, the dock master.

"Doing great. And you?"

"The same. Getting some work done?"

"Yes. We had some air in our line, and the engine kept cutting out."

Gabe stopped and grinned at me. "That typically happens when you run a tank dry."

"You're correct. That we did."

After some idle chat with the old guys, I wished them a good day and slowly walked back to our berth, looking for anything and anyone that seemed out of place. I saw nothing suspicious and returned to the boat as I finished my beer.

"What do you think?" asked Garry.

"Looks good to me. I didn't see anyone I'd worry about."

"Okay," said Garry, who left the cockpit and climbed below. "Let's do this," I heard him say through the hatch.

Our plan was to start transferring the weed from the boat to the vans, several bales at a time. It was common to see people on the docks with trash bags, laundry bags, and duffels, so if we moved slowly and didn't act weird, we weren't very likely to attract attention.

We filled a sail bag with the small bales. They were in five-kilogram bundles, wrapped in pink butcher paper and taped up with some brown packaging tape. A five-kilo bale was about the size of a concrete block and was tightly packed, weighing just over eleven pounds per bale. We could move about five at a time in the laundry bag, and another five or so in a sail bag that contained a spinnaker. Each filled bag weighed over fifty pounds, a bit awkward to lift with the bales loose inside a sack, but it was the only plan we had, and nobody had come up with any options. We'd take the sack up into the cockpit, put it beside us, sit down, look around the marina to see if anyone was paying attention, and then we'd casually get up and walk the bag to the van, which had its side doors open toward the sea, so nobody could see what we were doing as we unloaded the bales into the van and returned the bag to the boat.

We worked like this for over an hour, unloading over 1,000 pounds of weed in broad daylight, in plain sight for all the world to see, and nobody even paid attention. I could tell Garry was very impatient with the progress, and we tried to keep him calm. It was obvious that he felt exposed, and that's not something he liked at his level in the organization. Exposure to arrest was something grunts like me were expected to deal with, but not at his level, and he was not happy working at this level. I suspect the only reason he was exposing himself at this point was because of the man who'd come with him. The Colombian hitter was there to take control of the load, and Garry was the guy with his head on the block if anything went wrong. This was my first contact with any of the Colombians running the show. I would meet more in the coming weeks.

We began unloading much faster as we became comfortable and realized nobody was really paying attention. We finished up the first van, driven by the Colombian, and started loading the mechanic's van while he worked below on the engine.

I looked at Garry again. He was not enjoying himself. I can't say that for the rest of us. Mark, Jerry, and I were all buzzing with excitement. It was thrilling unloading the boat in broad daylight, and our hearts were beating fast. We kept looking at each other and grinning. It was fun and exciting, and there simply isn't any other way to describe it. We were working pirates, and we were loving it. Garry pulled me aside suddenly.

"Let's just get this shit off and be done," he said.

"What do you mean? We're doing fine. We have about another half hour at this pace."

"Let's just stop fucking around and unload it. I want to get the fuck out of here."

"What are you suggesting?" I thought I knew, but I wanted to hear him say it.

"Fuck the discretion. Let's just unload it like there wasn't anyone here. Nobody's paying attention. Let's cut the crap and just unload it."

"Garry . . ." I wasn't convinced. I was fine taking our time but also knew the longer we were doing it, the greater the chance of discovery by law enforcement.

"We're doing it." He'd made up his mind. He stuck his head down the hatch and told Mark and Jerry to just stuff as much in each bag as quickly as they could and start passing it up. No waiting, no looking around, just move it from the boat to the van as quickly as we could.

I wasn't happy with this decision, but once it was made, we all moved into high gear. The two men below stuffed five or six bales into each sack as quickly as it was emptied and tossed back to them, and we had a bucket-brigade chain between the cockpit and the van. We moved at a frantic pace, now expecting to get caught at any moment. Mark and I were laughing like maniacs as we worked. It was a rush, made more intense by the danger of getting caught. Within about ten minutes, we heard Garry say, "That's it!"

We stayed below while the mechanic left the boat and drove down the dock. He was taking a risk, but also knew there was a very nice payoff, the equivalent of a month's wages for two hours of his time. He had been instructed where to take his truck to transfer the load and headed for a nearby shed where Garry had parked a camper. As soon as the van had cleared the dock, we started looking out the portholes to see if anyone was watching us. We waited for several minutes, looking everywhere in the marina, but saw no one paying any attention to us.

Everyone else was gone—the mechanic and his van, and Garry and the Colombian in the other van. Mark, Jerry, and I casually walked up through the hatch, sat in the cockpit looking around, then moved off the boat as casually as we could. We walked down the dock at a slow pace, chatting and acting normal, until we reached the end of the dock. We quickly walked across a dirt parking lot and into a cluster of bushes and mangrove trees in the wooded lot next to the parking area. We stood back, out of sight, and watched our boat and the dock master's office for over half an hour. Nothing. Crickets. It appeared we were safe. The boat was unloaded, and we'd just completed our first smuggling trip. It was the first time in many weeks that I could finally take a deep breath and relax.

SIX

TAKING CARE OF BUSINESS

We returned to the boat and sat in the cockpit. Our next step would be to get it cleaned up to return to the charter company where Garry had leased it. There was loose weed and chaff everywhere, and the boat smelled strongly of it, so we hired a friend to come scrub it down with strong-smelling cleaners to get the smell out. We'd be in the marina for a few days, and then the plan was to return the boat to Miami and get our money. It seemed simple enough. We'd done the work, and now it was time to get paid.

Several problems quickly arose. I'd never negotiated any amount of money or pay for the trip, and neither had Mark and Jerry. We naively assumed that Garry would take care of us, and generously so, which was our first mistake. Our second mistake was making this run to Mexico in the first place, and we quickly learned that we'd put ourselves at risk for a shipment of crappy weed with almost no market value. We returned the boat, and I decided to hang around Coconut Grove and enjoy the wild nightlife. It seemed like a good way to pass the time while we were waiting to get paid. I hung out at Garry's condo with Mark and Jerry, and we slept on the couches. We assumed, incorrectly, that the money would be forthcoming as soon as the trip was over. We discovered within days that this wasn't to be the case, and Garry told us that he couldn't pay us until he sold the weed.

What he didn't tell us was something we already suspected. The weed that we'd brought back from Mexico was absolute garbage. It was low-grade, mostly leaves and stems, no large buds, and it even had pieces of corn husk and corn plants packed into the 5-kilo bales. We'd opened one on the return trip to sample and hadn't been very impressed. Now the weed was back in Miami and had been presented to the prospective buyer, who was rightly refusing to close the deal and hand over the money. After all we'd been through in the previous month, we weren't a happy bunch. We complained about it to Garry. At that point, I just wanted to go home and get back to my life.

"What are we going to do?" I asked him. "Isn't there someone who'll buy it cheap, just to take it off our hands?"

"The buyer we had lined up claims nobody will buy something that shitty," he said. "He's probably right. It's trash weed grown in corn fields for an extra buck. It's not something that came from a cartel-run operation. We got screwed."

I talked to Mark and Jerry and asked them what they thought. We all agreed that we'd be willing to take some of the weed as payment. I really didn't like the idea of having thirty or so kilos of weed in my possession, but at this point, I didn't see any other options for getting paid. The longer we waited for money, the better our chances of ending up with nothing, so we went to Garry and asked for our pay in product. He was quick to agree and seemed relieved that we were willing to quickly negotiate and move on. I was a bit shaggy from not having had a haircut in months, so I got a quick trim to look presentable and avoid any overt suspicion from law enforcement. I rented a car to get back to Key West, and I drove back down Highway One in a Ford Taurus with eight 5-kilo bricks of cheap Mexican weed in the trunk.

I'd hoped to be heading home with about twenty thousand dollars in cash—the going rate for smuggling captain in those days—but now I'd have to sell a bunch of cheap weed on my own to see a dime. After weeks of being stressed and thinking I'd be able to finally relax upon my return, I was now right back in the thick of things and had to be vigilant and always looking over my shoulder once again.

Upon returning to my apartment, I stashed the bales in my closet. I remember standing there, holding the closet door open, and looking at eight bales of weed stacked inside. I felt a strange mix of pride and trepidation. I felt like I'd accomplished something fun and cool that many people wanted to do but didn't have the balls to pull it off, but I was also worried about how I was going to move forty kilos of cheap weed to get my pay. I thought about making a deal to unload it all, but that would involve a big loss in revenue. Breaking it all down and selling it in pounds, quarter pounds, and ounces would take a lot longer, but would also ensure the largest return on the product. I calculated that if I was patient and sold it all to individuals, even at greatly reduced prices, I could still clear about fifteen thousand dollars, which would last me quite a while. I had no car, and my only expense other than groceries was my rent, which was $135 a month for my tiny studio apartment. At that moment, I decided to become a local drug dealer and see where it would take me. In the meantime, I wouldn't have to work, and I could hang out at the beach every day and go sailing on my friend's Hobie Cat, which he kept at Higgs Beach between the pier and the west Martello Tower fort. I didn't like the idea of having to become a dealer, but at least I wouldn't have to go back to a boring minimum-wage job.

The shortcomings of being a street-level dealer quickly became apparent. Like any good salesman starting with a new line of products, the first customers you go after are family and friends. I didn't have any family there, but I had lots of friends who were all more than happy to buy cheap Mexican weed. At the time, an ounce of good Colombian was around $30 to $50, and I was more than happy to sell a huge, overstuffed baggie of my Mexican yard trimmings for $20, so I had a steady business right from the start, selling ten to twenty bags a week to my friends and their friends. Some of my friends began asking for larger amounts at wholesale prices so they could sell on their own, and I was only happy to oblige because it insulated me from transactions with strangers. I knew it would cut down on my bottom line, but I really didn't care. I just wanted to keep the cash flow going and enjoy my new, somewhat carefree life as a smuggler and weed dealer.

As I mentioned earlier, when I first thought about being a smuggler, I never really thought of myself as a criminal. Smuggling just seemed like a fun and daring adventure on the high seas, and nothing more. Although I knew it was against the law, I never looked at it as being wrong in any moral sense. I was okay with that and made my peace with it. But dealing at the street level changed my view, and although I was enjoying the steady flow of cash and my new life, I was uncomfortable with the knowledge that I'd become a dealer. Even though it was only weed, I was nervous and troubled by what I had become out of necessity. I really wanted to move the product as fast as I could and be done with it.

The weeks passed and turned into months. My weed business had expanded, and suddenly, a lot of people I didn't know seemed to know that I was selling weed. I was approached by total strangers in local bars, asking to purchase weed. I pretended I didn't know what they were talking about until I established their connection to someone I knew. This made me very nervous, however, and it became increasingly common. Apparently, my friends were talking too much to their friends, and word was getting around. If I was known by this many strangers, how long would it be before someone in law enforcement came knocking? All the locals knew DEA guys hung around in local bars and clubs, pretending to be buyers. In most cases, they were easy to spot because they were so bad at their cover. They always traveled in pairs and looked like they'd both just walked out of a mall after purchasing cheap Hawaiian shirts and deck shoes. These guys were easy to spot, and we saw them everywhere, but we worried about the ones who were savvier, who worked alone and were good at their cover stories. It was those guys I worried about, not the rookies.

In an odd twist, while worrying way too much about my street deals, I was also taking a lot of unnecessary risks in other areas. When people wanted to buy weed, I often delivered it to their homes personally. I didn't want people to know where I lived, so I always offered home delivery. I never carried the weed on my person, but inside small brown paper grocery bags, like I was returning from a market. I also wore sneakers over my preferred sandals, but for a very good reason. I wanted to be able to run at a moment's notice, and I could easily ditch a small bag I was carrying rather than digging through my clothing for the weed. Several times a week, I'd find myself walking the streets of Key West carrying anywhere from an ounce to a quarter pound of weed in a small paper bag, right in public for everyone to see. Nobody in their right mind would do that, so it made perfect sense to be as public as possible while heading to my destination, and in the event that someone was following me, I was ready to run. I remember starting across Duval Street one day, jaywalking in the middle of the block, right in front of a police car that I hadn't noticed. He hit his brakes, and I stopped and panicked a bit before quickly regaining my composure. After a quick, angry glare from him, he nodded and waved me across in front of him. Sheepishly, I waved back, sighed in relief, and crossed the street with my bag of weed nestled in my arms. After that incident, I took side streets and stayed on the sidewalk when delivering my product.

After a few months, I had managed to stash quite a bit of cash in what I called my bank account, an old cigar box I kept in the cabinet above the refrigerator. My rent was paid ahead for six months, and I had several thousand dollars in cash on hand. I also lived right beside a Cuban bakery on Margaret Street, and at the end of every day when the delivery trucks returned, the drivers would put all the unsold bread on a rack at the back of the bakery. Locals in the know would stop by and take it for free. For me, it was a 50-foot walk from my back door to the bread rack, so I had free Cuban bread for all the years I lived on Margaret Street.

I finally reached a point where my nerves couldn't take it any longer. I was so well-known at that point that I was certain the wrong people had found out, and I would be busted. Things finally came to a head one evening when yet another total stranger knocked on my back door. He was a young guy with long hair, and we chatted for a bit before I figured out his connection to any of my friends. He wanted to buy a lot of my weed, and I was ready to let the remainder of it go for the right price. We sat down, smoked a joint, and worked out a price.

"When can you get the cash?" I asked. I think we'd agreed on about $1,000 for everything I had left, which was about three bales, or eighteen pounds.

"I might be able to get it tonight," he said.

"If you can get back here tonight with cash, I'll let it go for $800." A dumb move on my part, as he'd already agreed to $1,000. I wasn't the brightest businessman, but I was a practical one, and I wanted all the weed gone from my house as soon as possible.

His eyes lit up. "Seriously? That's no problem. I'll see you in a few hours."

For the next couple of hours, I sat in my house, filled with dread, fully expecting to be raided by the cops. Nothing happened, and right around sunset, he returned. I'd put everything into an old surplus Army duffel bag which I handed to him as he walked into the house. He pulled out eight nice, crisp, fresh $100 bills and counted them out into my hand. When I saw how nervous he was, I relaxed a bit and stopped worrying about him being with law enforcement. This was clearly the largest drug deal he'd ever done, and his heart was racing. He even stuttered nervously when talking to me before leaving, which relaxed me even more.

"Walk slowly when you hit the street," I told him. "Don't look like you're in a hurry. Just walk like some guy on his way to the laundromat, okay?"

"Okay. Will do. Thanks, man. Thanks!" He started down my sidewalk way too fast.

"Slow down!" I reminded him.

He turned, smiled, and slowed down. I never saw him again, and I was now free of all my weed. For the first time in many, many months, I felt free and unburdened. I poured myself a nice glass of 15-year-old Rhum Barbancourt Reserve, rolled up a joint of my garbage Mexican weed, and sat down on the back porch to relax. At that point, my first smuggling trip—and all that went with it—finally came to an end.

I had no idea what to do next. After spending the better part of a year with my life running at full speed, I was suddenly at a full stop, idling, and not knowing which direction to turn. Would I be offered another chance on another trip? Was this a case of one-and-done?

This was an era before cellphones and the internet and to stay in touch with someone required making telephone calls. I'd never had a telephone the entire time I lived in Key West. It was a small island, and if I wanted to see someone, I'd simply hop on my bicycle and ride to their house. If they weren't home or weren't able to visit, I'd make plans and come back at another time. Very few of my friends had telephones in their homes, and we all loved the culture of walking or riding to a friend's house for a visit, or even to just stop and make plans for another time. I think this aspect of American social culture has largely vanished with the arrival of the cellphone and instant access to anyone and everything via electronics. In any case, if I wanted to get in touch with Garry, I'd have to go to a payphone on the street somewhere with a pocketful of change and call him.

After a month of feeling aimless, I gave him a call. He was happy to hear from me and said he had some things in the works but wasn't specific. I'd quickly learned to talk in code when on the phone with him or Mark, so we had innocuous words we'd use in a conversation that wouldn't arouse any suspicion if the payphone was bugged. We'd been told that several of the pay phones in Key West were bugged because of ongoing law enforcement operations working on drug cases, so we safely assumed that the best course of action was to assume that they were all bugged and act accordingly.

I made plans to come visit, and since I had the cash, decided to fly on Air Sunshine, a small airline based in the Keys that still flew Cold War era Douglas DC-3 aircraft, a very sturdy, reliable twin-engine airplane that had been in continuous service around the world since World War 2. They were old, but safe, and it was an adventure flying in them. Air Sunshine operated between Tampa, Fort Lauderdale, Miami, and Key West and was the only air carrier that had aircraft small enough to land on the runway at that time. This was also before public anti-smoking laws, and the flights to Miami were very inexpensive, so it was fun to catch a quick flight to Miami and have a complimentary Miami Whammy (a dark rum drink with Cointreau and lime) while puffing a few Camel cigarettes in-flight.

Garry met me at the Miami airport in a beautiful white E-series BMW, which he hadn't owned before.

"Nice! Is this yours?" I asked.

"Sort of. A guy owes me some money he doesn't have. I'm driving his car until he pays me."

"Lucky you," I replied. This was a common practice, I'd learned. If you owe someone higher up within your crew, they hold your possessions for you until you pay. Most debt came from people using product (our name for cocaine) more than they should have, and getting behind on the money owed to the bosses. Some, as I learned, paid the ultimate price, but only if you messed up with the wrong bosses at the higher levels several times. Bottom line: If you owed someone and you couldn't come up with the money, you lost your expensive possessions, typically stuff you'd bought with money from selling drugs. Garry's condo had its share of expensive electronics, cameras, and gold jewelry from some of his crew who owed him money. He simply treated it as his, and he once told me that he rarely had to return any of it. Guys who were always in debt were users, and once they went down that rabbit hole, they rarely came back.

We headed to a nice neighborhood I'd never visited before and parked in the driveway. There was a realtor's sign in the front yard, suggesting the house was empty. Garry had a key and opened the door for me. I was nervous but shouldn't have been. I remember walking in and immediately looking to see if there were any plastic drop cloths spread out on the floor. I'd seen too many mob movies, and walking into an empty house first with Garry behind me made me nervous, although without just cause. It was simply a case of nerves. I knew I'd done a good job for him and brought in his load of crappy Mexican weed on schedule and without incident. I knew I was in good standing but still felt nervous walking into that house.

We went to the living room, and he motioned for me to have a seat on the couch before he walked to the kitchen at the back of the house. I heard the refrigerator open, and a sliding glass door open shortly after. Garry was talking quietly to someone, but I had no idea who it might have been, as he'd mentioned nothing on the ride from the airport. He returned to the living room with a beer for me, and another man walked in behind him. I stood to greet him, but he nodded and motioned politely for me to sit down. I sat back on the couch, and he sat in the chair next to me at the end of the coffee table.

He was about six feet tall and looked Hispanic. The one thing that stood out was his eyes.

They were probably brown, but I remember them looking almost black, which was unnerving. He was dressed in an expensive sports blazer with dress slacks and nice loafers, and he looked like a well-polished, well-to-do businessman. He reached out his hand after he sat down.

"How are you, Kelly? My name is Luis."

"I'm pleased to meet you," I replied. I'd heard Garry mention his name before. This was the head of the outfit he worked for, the highest-up member of the cartel that Garry knew on a personal level.

"I've been wanting to meet you. I've heard good things about you. Are you interested in more work with us?"

"Yes. Certainly. I really enjoy sailing and hope I can do more of that for you."

"Well, that's exactly what I had in mind. As I mentioned, you come highly recommended, so if you work with us, you'll be our captain, and you can pick your own crews. How does that sound to you?"

I was very happy to hear this. I knew I'd done a good job on the last trip, and this was a huge vote of confidence, particularly with the decision to let me pick my own crews. This was their way of letting me know that I was trusted to do a good job. I knew enough about the drug business in South Florida to understand the dynamics of getting involved with Colombians. If you showed any signs of being competent and trustworthy, you were quickly moved into positions of responsibility, and if you were a user who sometimes allowed your habit to control your actions, you might still be of use, but you were watched and not given responsibilities.

The one thing about Luis that I noticed immediately was his appearance and demeanor.

He looked very well-heeled, was sophisticated and well-dressed, and he possessed a genteel, relaxed personality. But behind those eyes, I could see a person who would be ruthless if crossed. We made some small talk, and then he leaned toward me and put his hand on my knee.

"Kelly, I need you to understand something important. Remember what I'm telling you right now. We work with a lot of people. If everyone does their job the way we expect, we're all happy. But sometimes people don't do the job we expect of them, or they step out of line and do something that's not in our interests. We make examples of those people, you know? It's unpleasant, but it's necessary. Do you understand?" He stared into my eyes, unblinking, for a long time. His mood hadn't visibly changed, but I sensed purposeful menace in his gaze.

I nodded yes.

"Tell me you understand what I'm saying. Say it out loud."

"I understand."

I met his gaze, and through eye contact let him know that I understood him completely. I already knew their code. Walk the line and do your job, and everything will be fine. Cross them in any way that damages their business, or puts them in contact with the law, and you were in trouble. You might survive the first time, but then you were deeply in their debt and would be forced to do dangerous jobs. Mess up again, and you were probably dead. After a long pause, he broke off eye contact, slapped my knee, and leaned back in his chair.

"Welcome aboard," he said. "I look forward to working with you."

He stood up, walked to the kitchen, and chatted quietly with Garry for a few moments, and then I heard the back door open and close. I walked to the kitchen and found Garry there alone. He grinned at me and nodded.

"That went well. He likes you and trusts you. That's a good thing. He'll work with anyone I bring in but generally doesn't want anything to do with them. But he liked you."

"Is Luis his real name?" I asked.

Garry laughed. "Now why would you ask that?"

"Just curious."

"No, but it's his name with the crew I work with. He works with about ten other crews, and they all know him by different names."

He went on to explain that most of the Colombians I'd meet within the organization all went by the name Luis. "There are two other guys named Luis you'll probably meet. It's by design."

I understood clearly. If I were arrested for anything and questioned, I'd be in no position to provide any reliable information if I knew nothing about the people I worked for, especially if they all shared the same first name and had no last names. It was a simple but brilliant way for him to create layers of insulation between himself and low-level employees like me. For the remainder of the time I worked for him, I never knew his real name, or his last name, and knew absolutely nothing about him or his family, other than that he was married and owned lots of restaurants and real estate.

To the outside world, Luis was a successful Colombian-American businessman. I learned from Garry that Luis's restaurants provided one of the ways he laundered his cash. With ten large, successful restaurants around Miami, it was easy to add many thousands of dollars to the cash drawer nightly, and once banked, it was clean money that could be used to grow his empire. With the clean money, Garry told me, Luis purchased homes and condos all over Miami, some of which sat empty for years while appreciating in value. He never used his own name to buy any property and instead used friends and low-level American business associates to complete straw purchases for him. Cash was king, and Luis had figured out how to prosper and increase his fortune while remaining almost invisible to anyone who tried to dig into his business dealings.

When Luis walked out the door that day, it would be the last time I ever saw him. I realized later that he spent very little time with low-level employees and only met with me to give me the speech about loyalty and expectations, and if I followed that code, it was the only time he'd ever have to meet with me. That, I realized later, was a very good thing.

"So, whose house is this?" I asked Garry.

"One of Luis's many homes."

"Is it really on the market?" I asked.

"No. He just leaves the sign out all the time. It's used primarily for a meeting house."

"But it's not in his name, I'm guessing."

Garry laughed again. "Of course not. Nothing is in his name. He's a ghost."

I was catching on.

"Your condo in Coconut Grove . . . is that yours, or his?"

Garry grinned and wagged his finger at me.

"Now you're getting it."

I was starting to see the bigger picture. One of the perks of being a mid-level guy for Luis was free housing in great neighborhoods. Garry was the equivalent of a made man with the Colombian cartel in Miami. In addition to being under their protection, he was the beneficiary of their penchant for collecting real estate and would always have a nice place to live while he worked for them.

On the drive back to Garry's condo, he explained that he had another trip planned, this time with two other men he wanted me to meet. They would be the primary sponsors of the trip, and Garry would be the organizer. Upon return, the shipment would be purchased by Luis's organization, trucked to the northeast where it would be sold to a local distributor.

The profits from the trip would be split down the middle. The two men who sponsored the trip would get half, and the other half would go to Garry and Luis. Smuggling was just wholesaling, purchasing a product from a supplier at a lower price, and then reselling it to a distribution network at a profit. We were just the middlemen between our buyers and street sellers. I wasn't certain who'd be paying the crew, so I asked.

"Don't worry about it," Garry told me. "Your pay is built into the deal."

A rather vague answer, and not one I wanted to hear.

This was the first time we spoke openly about pay. I was told I could pick my own crew, who'd each be paid $15,000. As the captain, I would be paid $30,000. If arrested, the organization would cover all our court costs, but there'd be no pay for the trip if the load was confiscated. But the best news was the destination. On this trip, we were going to Jamaica, a place I'd always dreamed of visiting someday. We'd sail down around the tip of Cuba, cut back east toward Jamaica, with a short stop in the Cayman Islands on the way. We also would have a bit more time to relax and have fun along the way, and we were allowed to take guests with us, who were free to accompany us to Jamaica, but would fly back home before we picked up our shipment. Everything about this trip sounded wonderful.

I was introduced to the two men who were doing some of the financial backing, and I couldn't have been more surprised when I met them. One was an older man about sixty years old, a West Texas rancher who'd done well for himself. He had some money to play with it seemed and wanted to get in on the action in South Florida. The other, his friend, was a younger man who had a thing for loud Hawaiian shirts and aviator glasses. He had a big mustache, sandy blonde hair, and looked like he probably drank too much. I'd been expecting Colombians for some reason, so meeting up with two midwestern white males who looked like they'd be at home selling Cadillacs in Amarillo caught me off guard. Ed was the older gentleman, and Rick was the younger one. They might have even been related, but I can't recall all the details. They had requested to meet with the captain, and Garry set up the meeting. We met in Coconut Grove at a club called Taurus, which was a wild spot on the weekends. Ed and Rick looked out of place, but they quickly took a liking to it. I got the impression that they had a preconceived idea of South Florida social life, and this was living up to their expectations.

Ed was a true gentleman, and naturally a bit nervous about putting up thousands of dollars without meeting all the players. He wasn't worried about who I would choose for the crew. He just wanted to meet the man who'd be responsible for the load once it left Jamaica, and he seemed content with me after I answered all his questions. I hadn't expected someone like him to be involved in this business, and I'm pretty sure he didn't expect someone like me to be involved, either. I still had a clean-cut preppy look at the time, and I noticed it opened a lot of doors for me in a business where most people expected to meet hardened criminals and jaded drug dealers, not wide-eyed, clean-cut kids who looked like they'd stepped out of a prep school.

After talking to Ed, I was impressed and had a good feeling about the trip. I didn't want a repeat of the first one, where nothing was planned, and we just flew by the seat of our pants daily. His friend Rick seemed to be along for the ride, and I found out later he'd been the one who introduced Ed to Garry, so he was in for a cut as a finder's fee, but not a full cut as a cash sponsor.

Back in Key West, I quickly got in touch with one of my best friends and asked him if he'd be interested in being one of my crew members. Greg jumped at the chance and suggested another guy he knew named Jack. I'd never met Jack, but I took Greg's word for it. Greg was a rock-solid character, and someone I'd trust with my life. He was a first-generation American-Ukrainian from the Chicago area and had moved there when his family left Ukraine when he was still a young child. He spoke English as well as Ukrainian and loved to make Polish food. He was dating a younger woman at the time but decided not to take her on the trip. His friend Jack had an English girlfriend who'd be joining us, and we all met for drinks at the Half Shell Raw Bar so that Jack and I could get to know each other. He seemed like a rough character, and I learned he'd done some jail time, which made me a bit nervous. He didn't seem very laid back, but I trusted Greg, so I welcomed him to the crew.

The plan was simple. Garry had a boat lined up in Miami that we would charter for a month for $12,000, a nice piece of change in 1982. I met the young owners, a young sailing couple who seemed to know what we were up to, but didn't ask any questions, and seemed more than willing to take their chances to make that kind of money. Typically, you could rent a 40-foot sailboat for about $500 to $700 a week in those days, so our willingness to overpay for the lease was a dead giveaway about our real intentions.

Garry had me charter the boat in my own name, and I was listed on the lease as the captain and sole member of the lease party. This created some liability for me if caught, which is why I was making twice what the crew would be making. Much like our trip to Mexico, we would not be applying for a departure manifest from US Customs but would simply sail to Jamaica and check in with Jamaican customs upon our arrival. The plan called for us to sail first to Grand Cayman Island, where we'd hang out several days in the harbor, playing the part of young, well-to-do sailors. On this trip, Garry's girlfriend would be joining us, so we'd have Jack's girlfriend Susan, and Garry's live-in girlfriend Sarah. Apparently, Bebe, the other girlfriend on the West Coast, had been under the impression that Garry was giving up Sarah for her, and when that didn't materialize, she moved on, and we never saw her again. Sarah seemed like a good soul who liked the lifestyle she was living but was smart enough to know it came at a cost. She was savvy and seemed to know that she had a window in which to enjoy her lifestyle, one that she was certain wouldn't last long. She was also fiercely loyal to Garry, even though I'm certain he wasn't fiercely loyal to her. She would be acting in the same capacity as Bebe on this trip, which was to be the ears and eyes for Garry, who never sailed with us except on short day sails when we were in a port.

From the first mention of the trip until our departure, things moved very smoothly. Everything was planned for us by Ed and Rick, and every step was executed like clockwork. It was easy to see that Ed had managed operations before and knew how to make certain every step happened right on schedule. Our last night in Key West was a fun one. We all went to dinner at the Pier House down on Mallory Square, and ran up a huge tab. Whatever we wanted, Ed told us. I think our final tab was around $800, a huge dinner tab in the early 1980s, and at least half of the tab was expensive champagne and rare Scotch.

We set sail from Oceanside Marina the next day on a 42' Tartan sloop, a fast and nimble boat that the owners occasionally raced. It was beautifully equipped, with three different jibs and a spinnaker.

"Like a real sailboat," I told everyone.

This was a boat that would go anywhere and get there quickly. It was a joy to sail, but as it didn't have autopilot or air conditioning, we'd have to keep hatches open for fresh air below, and someone would always have to have their hands on the wheel.

I broke the days up into 4-hour watches, around the clock. Each of us—me, Greg, and Jack—4 hours on watch, then 8 hours off to sleep or do whatever you wanted. We'd each have daylight and a night watch. I took the first watch upon leaving port, and during the day, everyone spent most of their time lying on the deck or hanging out in the cockpit. Within a few days, our watches had become routine, and we fell into the rhythms of the sea. Sarah stayed awake on my watch with me, Jack and Susan kept company on Jack's watch, and Greg was usually all on his own during his night watch, so I requested he wear the harness and clip himself to the safety line in case he slipped overboard at night while we were all sleeping.

The sleep arrangements were awkward at first, but we worked out the details within a few days. There was only one full-time double cabin, which was in the bow. The remainder of the bunks were singles, and although the dining table could be dropped to create another double, we didn't want it taking up space in the main cabin. Greg took one of the single bunks that stretched back under the cockpit. Jack and Susan used the double bunk when I was on watch, and then I slept up there with Sarah when Jack and Susan took their night watch.

Sarah was quick to let me know that we were just sharing the large double bunk out of necessity, and she slept on one side with pillows between us. I confess I had a hard time sleeping with a beautiful woman lying next to me in shorts and a swim top, but I managed. After a night or two in this arrangement, we grew comfortable with the situation and often talked quietly for long periods while lying side by side in the bunk. I liked her. She was a sweet woman, and we got along just great. Like Bebe, she trusted me and always spoke highly of me to Garry. I know this because Garry used to tell me so, often kidding around and asking me if I was paying them to say nice things about me. Sarah was always asking me why I didn't have a girlfriend.

"I don't know," I told her. I really didn't know.

I had lots of female friends I spent time with, but none that I dated regularly or exclusively. In every case, it was mutual. They seemed to want to keep their personal freedom as much as I did, although there were several I would have happily dated exclusively if they'd requested it. But it was Key West in the 1980s, and few people my age wanted to be tied down. Living the island life was all about freedom, free love, and grand dreams. After a while I just surrendered to the island vibes and rolled with the punches.

"But don't you want anything more? I do. I don't think Garry will ever marry me, but as long as we're together, I'm going to have that as my goal."

"Good luck on that," I said. "Doesn't it bother you that he still has a wife and kids that he loves, but won't live with, and at least one more girlfriend that he won't commit to?"

"Sure. But I love him, and he loves me. I know that much."

I couldn't disagree on that. Even though Garry kept the two or three women in his life on a short rope, it was also obvious that he really cared about Sarah. Despite the crassness of having three relationships going at once, it was clear that he cared for her very much. But I found myself bringing up the matter more often, almost daily. I was becoming attracted to her myself and wanted to see if I could weaken her resolve a bit. It was difficult sleeping beside her every night without feeling something for her, especially after our nightly conversations.

Although she was loyal to Garry, I could tell she enjoyed my attention and flirted with me often. I liked it and responded. Greg noticed and warned me to take it easy.

"Haven't you learned anything about workplace dating?" he asked.

I just laughed. I didn't care at that point. If an opportunity presented itself, I was going to take it.

After a day of sailing, we were ready to round the western tip of Cuba and turn east toward the Cayman Islands. We were cautious to stay well offshore, but the mountains along the coast of Cuba loomed large and seemed closer than the fifteen miles shown on the LORAN. I saw a few larger boats, and assumed they were fishing boats, but just to be safe I turned on the engine and motored back out into the Gulfstream. I had tried to stay as close to the coast as possible to avoid the strong current but figured it was safer to spend some extra fuel than end up with a confiscated boat sitting in a Cuban jail somewhere.

We turned the corner, sailed out of the Yucatan Channel, and into the Caribbean at last. We felt the steady winds moving from slightly north of East, and we'd spend the next several days on a port tack with steady 15 knot winds. It was Caribbean sailing at its best. The days were balmy with a slight overcast, and we quickly settled into the mellow sailing, playing music, drinking rum, smoking weed, and doing some coke. We'd have to use it all up before getting to the Cayman Islands, so if we weren't on our watch, we were either partying on deck, or down below in our berths sleeping it off. Greg told me later that I always seemed to have a grin on my face during that trip. I wasn't surprised to hear that. Everything seemed to be going perfectly, and I had a good feeling it would continue to for the remainder of the trip.

The first leg of our trip to Grand Cayman went off without a hitch. After several days of perfect sailing in perfect weather, we dropped anchor in Georgetown harbor, a gorgeous lee shore with crystal-clear water with hundreds of feet of visibility. We were amazed by the clarity, and while waiting for Customs to clear us, we put on our snorkels and jumped over the side. It was amazing, and floating on the surface in the clear water felt like we were flying. We cleared Customs quickly, and went ashore for a cocktail at an old, classic British-style pub named The King George that was on a road facing the harbor. We sat at the outside tables, toasted to a successful voyage, and decided to take a few days to enjoy the local island life. We had no set arrival time for Jamaica, and we'd given ourselves several extra days during planning for things such as bad weather and enjoying life ashore. On this trip Garry would be flying ahead of us and meeting us in Jamaica, so we were on our own for several days on the island of Grand Cayman.

The British flavor of the island was interesting, and we chatted with a lot of British expatriates who'd moved there from England. Most of the ones we met were single men who drank too much and seemed a bit cranky about life in general. We encountered them everywhere, running bars and restaurants, rental shops, and other businesses. On our second day we rented mopeds and explored the western coast, but Sarah kept pushing us to shorten our stay and push on to Jamaica. I'd been told a storm was brewing and wanted to wait it out, but she said she'd spoken to Garry on the phone, and he was impatient and didn't want us dallying around in the Caymans. During breakfast, I pulled Jack, Greg, and Susan aside to let them know.

"Sorry, guys. We must move on. Garry's getting impatient."

"Fuck him," said Jack. "What's an extra day or so? We've been sailing for almost a week." Jack and Jerry hadn't warmed to each other, and neither pretended to like the other.

"We're employees. We work for him. We must get going."

"Can we spend the rest of the day at least?"

"I don't see why not. There's supposed to be a storm moving through. Maybe it will have passed by then."

"Cool. Then let's have some fun today," said Susan. She was a bright, sunny person, and I could never figure out what she was doing with Jack, who seemed like a dark, angry character.

We spent the rest of the day enjoying the beach, the sun, and the pubs, and toward sunset we pulled anchor, raised the sail, and headed north around the tip of Grand Cayman. We'd be sailing between Grand Cayman Island and the other smaller islands, Little Cayman and Cayman Brac, on our course for Montego Bay, Jamaica. Throughout the evening, the weather was pleasant, and we ran a port tack for most of the night. I started to think that the storm warnings had been a false alarm and began to relax a bit after being on edge all night. It was dark, with no moon, and I couldn't see much of the sky, but I had learned to trust my senses when at sea, and I could notice slight shifts in anything, such as the wind, the smells, the feel of the air. If anything changed slightly, I could sense it. So far, I'd sensed nothing out of the ordinary.

Suddenly, with absolutely no warning, the wind just stopped dead. The sails went slack. The temperature dropped several degrees, and the air smelled strange. We were about to get slammed. I screamed down the hatch to get Greg and Jack on deck as quickly as possible. Before they even cleared the hatch, the storm slammed us full force, the wind going from still to about 40 knots is just seconds. As Jack and Greg made their way to the mast, I screamed for them to hold on. Neither was wearing a safety harness, and if they'd been knocked overboard at night without a life vest in the storm, I'd never find them.

The waves picked up immediately and the bow began lifting out of the sea at steep angles and falling back with a thud. I cranked up the motor to get some speed going so I could steer the boat while Jack and Greg stowed the sails. It seemed like they were on the front deck forever but finally managed to drop and stow the jib and lower the mainsail to secure it. Since I had the only harness and lifeline, I told them to stay below, but keep an eye on me. I kept the motor running while the storm front moved through, and after about half an hour of very rough sailing, the winds began to drop to about 25 knots. The seas remained rough, the waves still high, but things finally stabilized. I tied myself to the tiller post with some rope, had Greg put on my harness, and had him go forward to run up the storm jib, a very small triangle that would help keep us moving forward, and then had him put up a reefed mainsail. Once we were completely under sail again, I turned off the motor. We began to move quickly, about seven or eight knots, even with the greatly reduced sail area. The boat pitched and rolled wildly, but we were moving and making great time. I had everyone stay below unless the boat's motion really bothered them, and if they came into the cockpit, I had them tie some rope to their waist and then tie off the other end to some anchor point on the boat. It was still very rough, and hard to stand in the cockpit without bracing yourself, and I didn't want anyone slipping overboard.

The heavy winds and waves lasted through the night, and as the morning approached, both the wind and waves began to settle down. The clouds steadily parted, giving way to clear sky above, and as the sun rose over the Caribbean, we once again raised the larger jib, took the reefs out of the main, and settled into a lovely starboard tack that would take us north of the island. I'd been too busy during the night to take our position and knew that we were off course a bit during the night, but I knew we wouldn't be off by much. I checked our position, learned we were farther north than planned, so we tacked and began running south southeast, on a course for Montego Bay.

For years, I'd dreamed of visiting Jamaica by sailboat, and that dream was about to come true. About an hour after sunrise, I looked ahead and was startled to suddenly see mountains rising from the sea. I took a deep breath and stared ahead, filled with emotion. It was one of the most beautiful sights I'd ever seen from a boat. As we moved forward, the hills came into better view, and I could make out more details and hear isolated sounds even when we were still about five miles offshore. It always struck me as odd how certain sounds carried across the water while others didn't. I heard a cow mooing. I heard what sounded like someone banging a pot. I heard a motorcycle accelerating. I heard a child shout. And then, as we came within a mile of the harbor, I heard more sounds, until at last, as we entered the harbor and were surrounded by the hillsides of Montego Bay, my ears were filled with a cacophony of sounds, an orchestra of life, of noise, of civilization. It was magical, and I remember having a big grin on my face all the way through the harbor and into our slip at the Montego Bay Yacht Club.

SEVEN

JAMAICA

When most people think of a yacht club, what often comes to mind is a slick, spiffy and expensive waterside venue like a country club on the water, the docks filled with pricey motor yachts, with bluebloods walking the docks sipping gin martinis. The Montego Bay Yacht Club was not any of those things, and I was relieved. It was pure funk and looked like something from a movie set. Just one long rickety dock, with lots of smaller slips, leading to a bar and run-down clubhouse at the shore. The bar had an open end that faced the harbor, the perfect place to sit and have a drink. The mood was extremely casual and run by an old rummy with a British accent.

After tying up and heading ashore, where we contacted Customs to clear port, we immediately parked ourselves at the bar and ordered a round of Red Stripe beer.

After soaking in the atmosphere, I looked around the bar. Nearly every patron in the place looked exactly like we did . . . disheveled, poorly groomed, and dressed in shorts and t-shirts. I loved it. This place was full of offshore sailors and local drunks, and we immediately felt right at home. While Greg, Jack, Susan, and I had a drink, Sarah found a phone and got in touch with Garry, who'd arrived at the island a few days earlier and was staying at a nice resort hotel on Richmond Hill, which overlooked the harbor. He'd arrived with Ed and Rick, and the three of them wanted us to come up to the hotel for dinner on our first night ashore in Jamaica.

A local Customs officer arrived at the Yacht Club and cleared us for entry, and since we had the day to relax before heading up to Richmond

Hill for the evening, we did our laundry at the club, had a few more drinks, and then fell asleep in some deck chairs on the dock. Around five that evening, we got cleaned up, put on our best clothes, and took a cab through the streets of Montego Bay on our way to the resort.

The single thing that I remember of the cab ride was the closeness of the streets, the tightly packed people, and the noise. We made the trip through town with the windows down, and for the entire trip, there was constant music drifting from homes, other cars, and bars, mixed with the sounds of very vocal people everywhere. They always seemed to be talking, singing, or shouting. I'd never seen anything like it before, even in small Mexican towns from the previous trip. If I had to recall just one single thing about the island, it would be that. During the day, no matter where we were, it was rarely quiet. Music was always playing somewhere, like it was part of the DNA of the island life, and the island could not survive without it.

We finally turned up the drive to the resort at Richmond Hill, and it was like driving into a different world. One second, we were surrounded by the sounds of the street, teeming with life, and in a matter of a minutes, we were climbing out of the cab into a genteel, subdued setting, the sounds of the neighborhood temporarily squelched and nullified. It was a beautiful resort, but I felt uneasy for some reason. I preferred the environment I'd just left and felt out of place in the one I'd just entered.

We found our way to the bar, which was open to the west and overlooked Montego Bay. It was an incredible sight, and one I'll never forget. We ordered drinks while waiting for Garry, Ed, and Rick, and I took the opportunity to walk to the edge of the patio. The bar was built right on the edge of the hillside, with steep drop-offs on three sides. There was a small rock wall around the edge of the patio, and I walked to it and looked down over. Directly below, at the bottom of the hillside, was a shantytown, filled with tightly-packed dwellings, barely larger than garden sheds, with people living in them. It covered the hillside, and there must have been thousands of people packed into a few acres. I was instantly filled with a sense of guilt for having more than them, and once I'd seen it, I could not unsee it. It made me uncomfortable, and I found myself in a subdued mood for the rest of the evening. I couldn't stop thinking about people having to live like that while I dined on lobster and steak above them. I could not enjoy myself knowing what was right below.

Nobody else seemed the least bothered by it, and they all enjoyed their dinner on the patio. I admit that it was a grand affair with one of the most incredible views I'd ever witnessed while dining. Garry and Ed were in great spirits, and as we dined, we went over the details for the pickup. We would be leaving in two days to sail down the coast to a small inlet known as Discovery Bay. We'd anchor in the harbor, stay on the boat, and wait for confirmation of the pickup. That evening, we'd sail offshore, just outside the harbor, and two skiffs would arrive with the load. Unlike the Mexican trip, these bales would be much larger, about 40 pounds each, wrapped in waterproof butcher paper, then wrapped again with burlap and taped up. The burlap was simply there to create friction so the stacked bales wouldn't slide around as much as they would have if stacked in butcher paper. Plus, it made them easier to grip and hold when moving and provided a layer of protection if the paper was ripped or punctured.

Having one trip under my belt, I already felt like a pro at everything. I noticed how Garry and Ed asked me lots of questions, and even though I was barely twenty-four at the time, they clearly deferred to me and trusted my opinion on anything related to the boat, the course I was choosing, and my projected time for returning to the Keys. It made me feel good to be trusted and treated like one of them. Throughout the dinner, Ed called me Captain instead of Kelly, which I liked hearing.

"What do you think about this, Captain?" he'd ask when going over plans. I loved hearing it and couldn't get enough.

After dinner I ordered another beer, walked to the stone wall encircling the patio, and sat on the edge sipping my beer and staring down into the shantytown. It unnerved me and bothered me to watch humans living in such squalor and poverty, while I sat above them, clean and well-fed, and in a position to do nothing for them while plotting to enrich myself to better enjoy life.

We took a cab back to the Yacht Club later that evening and had the cab driver take us downtown to some of the clubs frequented by tourists. They were exactly what we expected them to be and didn't stay long. On the last leg back to the marina, the cabbie offered us a large fistful of very high-quality weed for $3 Jamaican. The same amount in the States would have been ten times that amount. I made a note to myself that if the opportunity arose, I was going to make a deal of my own for something this good, as insurance.

The next two days in the marina were idyllic and fun. We sailed around the bay, following another sailboat crewed by some young people we'd met in the Yacht Club. They were a fun bunch and weren't smugglers, but they knew what we were up to and joked about it.

Although we trusted them, we never let on that they were correct in their assumptions. After restocking the boat with everything we'd need for the return trip, we said goodbye to Susan and Sarah, who'd be flying back to the States with our cameras and film. We took lots of photos on the trip down but did not want any photos of what took place after we picked up. Why provide additional evidence to prosecutors if we were caught?

The sail to Discovery Bay was uneventful and relaxing. We pulled into the harbor area in the late afternoon and dropped anchor. It was a beautiful little bay and could have easily graced a travel book cover. It was lush and green in every direction. The hillsides rose up steeply behind it, and we could hear the sounds of small-town life as we sat on the boat and relaxed. We quickly grew bored just sitting on the boat waiting for evening to fall, so we took the dinghy ashore to see the town. We had no plans or distinct purpose for going ashore other than to satisfy our curiosity. We walked a few streets close to the harbor, chatted with a few kids who cracked jokes about us being smugglers, had a few beers in a small bar, and watched a Rastafarian with pounds of dreadlocks piled on his head roll up a large blunt with newspaper and smoke it. I looked into his eyes and could see he was on another plane of reality than the rest of us. He looked at me, but I got the impression he was so high he wasn't seeing me.

"Mon. Do you have any paper?"

I wasn't sure what he meant. "What do you mean?" I asked.

"Paper. Do you have paper?"

I was still confused.

"I guess so," I replied. "What type do you need?"

He laughed. "Any paper, mon. Paper is paper."

I explained that we had newspapers, cardboard wrappers, letter-sized paper . . . all sorts of paper.

His eyes lit up, and he smiled. "Yes, some papers would be good. Can I have some? I'm running out of newspapers." He held up the blunt he was smoking and pointed at it.

It finally dawned on me that he needed papers for rolling weed. He explained that it was almost impossible to get any type of thin paper for rolling, and he used whatever he could find, including dried plant leaves. I went back out to the boat and gathered up several sheets of paper laying around, threw in a small tablet, and grabbed him a few packs of my Zig-Zag rolling papers. He was stunned when I returned with the bag of goodies, and I thought he was going to cry when he saw two packs of real rolling papers.

He thanked me profusely, and for a few moments, I'd made a new friend. We hung around the shore for a bit longer and then decided to head back to the boat for the evening. We had a few more beers, smoked a joint, and took a nap until sunset.

Shortly after dark, we watched the shoreline in town. If everything was set and ready to do, Garry would signal us with three blinks of a green light from shore. We used a colored light just to make sure we didn't mistake someone else's light for our signal light. If anything had gone wrong and we needed to wait another night, there would be no signal and we'd just sit tight for another day. About thirty minutes after dark, we saw a blinking green light on shore. Three flashes. A long pause. Three more flashes. Our response was to blink the running lights on the bow and top of the mast. It was on. We were good to go.

My pulse quickened just like it had in Mexico as we pulled anchor and headed out of the harbor. This would be our last exposure to danger from law enforcement or criminals until we reentered US waters. One of the strange things about smuggling on boats was that danger could come at you from two different fronts. You always had to worry about law enforcement and worry about getting hijacked by people not associated with the crew you worked for. Criminals in the drug trade were notorious for going after unprotected targets, and a sailboat from the States with three guys and a ton of weed would have been an easy target for someone who knew about us and was a rival of the gangs who were supplying us. Once we were loaded and underway back to the States on the open sea, we'd be safe for a week or so. I hadn't made as much money off the last trip as I'd hoped, so I really wanted this trip to go smoothly. So far, it had, and I was going to take every precaution to make sure it continued to do so.

It was another dark night, just like in Mexico, with no moon out, and when we were still over the sandy bottom outside the bay, I dropped anchor. There was a bit of a swell that night, and the boat was rising and falling a bit more than I would have liked. It would make for a difficult transfer having a skiff tied off to the side of the sailboat. We'd just have to deal with it.

After about fifteen minutes at anchor, we heard the first skiff coming. We couldn't tell exactly where they were coming from, but it sounded as though they had loaded the skiffs somewhere inside the bay. The first skiff arrived, and after a few grunts and nods of acknowledgement, the men on the skiff started throwing the bales into the cockpit, and I passed them down through the hatch to Greg and Jack, who stacked them in the bunks. The Tartan sloop was quite a bit smaller than the 52-foot Morgan we'd used in Mexico, and the space filled up quickly. Other than the forward bow cabin and single bunk under the cockpit by the navigation station, there was no place to lie down, or even sit. Every other empty space on the boat was stuffed with bales. Unlike the tightly wrapped 5-kilo bundles we'd dealt with in Mexico, these larger bales were not well-sealed, and the strong odor of marijuana filled the cabin. It didn't smell bad, but it smelled strong, and anyone who came close to the boat would be able to smell it as well. I had developed a strong ability to deal with any situation and make the best of it, so I noted the strong smell and planned to steer clear of other boats, especially when we arrived back in Key West. I was beginning to use the phrase "it is what it is" quite often. I couldn't control the situations, but I could control how I personally accepted each situation.

The first boat finished up, pulled away, and made room for the second boat. Greg and Jack were very wound-up and nervous, but I was relatively calm. I'd already been through this experience once, and this time around, I wasn't nervous or excited. It was just business, and I found time to relax and enjoy the experience, to remove myself from the immediacy of the moment, and drift above it. I felt like my mind was taking pictures for later, and I had time to reflect and frame the images, rather than rush the experience.

With the last bale on board, we waved goodbye to the Jamaicans, lifted our anchor, turned downwind, and raised the sails. It was an exhilarating sensation as the air filled the sails. We were on a downwind run for the next few days, and it would be the easiest sailing of the trip. We ran wing-and-wing, with the main set on one side of the mast and the jib on the other. It was a lovely, steady breeze, unchanging in direction, so we used the spinnaker pole on the jib for more stability, and for the next two days, we surfed our way toward the Yucatan Channel.

EIGHT

DEEP WATERS

Open water sailing was the one single part of smuggling that I loved more than anything else. It didn't matter if we were on our way to the pickup, or on our way home. I loved being at sea, taking my watch, and getting into the rhythm of the open ocean. There is nothing to compare it to, although it is a singular experience that's not for everyone. I'd been at sea with people who couldn't enjoy it and couldn't wait to get back to shore. To them, it was a means to get somewhere, and nothing more. To me, it was the entire reason I was doing what I was doing. The sailing was the most important part of the trip. Any money I would make, and any fun I might have on the trip, came as the result of the fact that I was a competent sailor who could go to sea and return, and any money I made was to be used to get my own boat so I could eventually do it whenever I wanted, whenever the mood struck me.

My plan on this trip was to take the same evasive actions I'd taken on the last trip. Rather than round the western tip of Cuba and take advantage of the 3-knot Gulfstream, I'd take us across the Yucatan Channel just offshore of the Mexican coast, being careful to stay in international waters. We'd sail up the coast of the Yucatan, up high into the Gulf of Mexico, and once again approach Key West from the northeast, where we'd blend in with the fishing fleet and not attract attention. The Coast Guard focused most of their efforts in the Straits of Florida between Cuba and the Keys, so we'd be out of the route commonly used by smugglers. I'd known other smugglers who took a different route by leaving Jamaica and sailing north through the gap between Cuba and Haiti and then skirt the coast of Cuba all the way back to the Keys. If we'd been unloading in the upper Keys, or anywhere close to Miami, this route would have made more sense, but I also knew it was heavily watched and had much more traffic. I felt our route would be the safest and least traveled.

The two days of downwind sailing were pure heaven. We barely spoke, and only when it was necessary. It's not that we were being antisocial, but there was simply no need for it. When you're on a small boat at sea with other people, you create a bubble for yourself and exist within it. It can be rough being in close quarters with the same people around the clock for weeks, so you learn how to isolate yourself. You filled your time with books, music (we'd brought a guitar, and there was a tape deck on the boat), communing with the ocean and its environment, and cooking your own meals to your own liking. The only communal time happened organically, and it was typically around sunset that we'd all be on deck at the same time, enjoying a good rum cocktail, smoking a joint, and chatting about nothing in particular. Life at sea was simple and perfect. You were away from all the worries and daily troubles of life on land. You understood that it was a temporary situation, so you squeezed everything you could out of the experience.

Although I'd never spent time at sea with Greg or Jack, they both fell into open water life very quickly.

After a few days we found ourselves approaching the Yucatan peninsula, well below the island of Cozumel. After a course adjustment and finally trimming the sails in a new position, we headed north, carried by the strong Gulfstream current, and averaging about 9 knots. The winds remained gentle, and we ran under full sail.

It was in the Yucatan Channel, just north of Cozumel, that I experienced one of the most profound encounters of my life. It was early morning, and I'd been on watch since 3 AM. I'd be replaced by Greg at 6 AM, so I smoked a joint while drinking an espresso I'd made minutes earlier. The sky was just growing light on the eastern horizon, and the entire sky filled with a pale peach color. I was looking aft and suddenly saw a pilot whale leap out of a wave and surf down the front. And then another. And another. As I watched, the entire ocean behind me began to boil with pilot whales, leaping out of every wave, and all heading toward me. Within thirty seconds the entire boat was surrounded by a huge pod of pilot whales.

Pilot whales are part of the dolphin family, but are much larger, and look something like a solid black Orca. I realized that they were breaching to get a better view of me and the boat. I was shaking with excitement and couldn't believe what I was experiencing. There must have been one hundred or more of them, and they were jumping out of the water surrounding the boat. Several come up very close, and as they arced through the water, they'd roll sideways and make eye contact. I had never experienced anything that intense in my life.

Over the next minute, at least twenty different members of the pod came alongside the boat, rolled on their sides, and made prolonged eye contact. I found myself shaking, with tears in my eyes, completely lost in the moment. They were tears of joy and amazement, coming from the realization that I'd just witnessed something incredibly unique, and that only a handful of people had ever experienced. Once the pod seemed satisfied with their close-up inspection of me and the boat, they stopped breaching but followed the boat for several more minutes. The experience remains vividly stamped on my brain, and one I'll never forget.

The remainder of the trip went smoothly without incident. With Ed and Rick at the helm of the operation, everything was planned out well in advance, and we weren't flying by the seat of our pants as we had been on the first trip to Mexico. We'd been told before we left that there'd be a crew of people with fast boats to unload us right offshore at night, rather than take the risk of pulling into a marina and unloading. I also knew that the Marine Patrol and Coast Guard always looked for suspicious boats lurking around and trying to stay out of sight, so I took the opposite approach and decided to hide in plain sight. When we returned to the Keys, I sailed the boat right to the Casa Marina Hotel, the most exclusive resort hotel in Key West, dropped anchor, sealed up the hatches so the smell wouldn't alert anyone, and we went ashore and drank some cocktails at the outdoor bar, pretending like we'd just been on a day sail. We called Garry and Ed, and they made plans to meet us at a local restaurant for lunch. As we finished our cocktails, I looked out at the Tartan sitting at anchor with some other sailboats around it, looking completely at home and not the least bit suspicious. Who in their right mind would anchor a sailboat with two thousand pounds of weed right in front of the Casa Marina? I was proud of myself to the point of being too cocky, but I just knew everything would be okay on this trip. I was right, but this cockiness would get me in serious trouble in a few months.

Everything moved quickly. Over lunch we were told that the local crew would unload us that evening. We'd sail offshore a few miles, and the smaller speedboats would come out and take our load. Once empty, we'd sweep up any loose weeds on the boat, spray everything with Lysol, and sail into Oceanside Marina once again, this time completely empty. And that's exactly how it went.

A few hours after sunset, we paddled out to the boat as if we were retiring for the night. We sat on deck, had a beer, and watched the patio at the resort for any signs of people who might be watching us. After seeing nothing that aroused our suspicion, we pulled anchor and headed offshore a few miles under engine power. We had our running lights on, but the guys who were to take our load were way ahead of us and had watched us leave the resort. We heard their motors nearby in the dark, but they had no running lights, as the sight of a sailboat at night with two smaller boats around it might arouse suspicion if any law enforcement was watching from shore. They tied up on each side of us, and within twenty minutes we'd emptied the boat of our load. Still running without lights, the speedboats left us and headed for Boca Chica Channel between Stock Island and Boca Chica. They'd go under the bridge to the north side of the island, and unload at a remote spot, where a camper would be waiting to take the load. Garry and Ed had hired a young couple to take the camper and drive it to a city in the northeast, where it would be sold directly to a group affiliated with Garry's people. A young, affluent-looking couple in a Winnebago wouldn't attract attention, and they'd used this formula many times before with success. We'd been told that it might be a week or so before we were paid, but we were comfortable and realized we didn't have any choice in the matter.

After unloading, we quickly swept up any chaff and loose weed laying around the boat, and threw it overboard, along with any personal stash we might have, just in case we were boarded in the marina. After spraying everything down with Lysol and giving the interior a quick wipe-down, we pulled into Oceanside Marina again, but this time right in front of the dock master's office. It was officially closed for the day, but quite often the dock master would hang around and drink beer with residents of the marina, as he was this evening. Gabe watched us pull in, taking one of our bowlines, and we signed up for a slip. I didn't see anyone suspicious hanging around, so we moved the boat to our slip, tied up, and sat down in the cockpit. Greg and I were relaxed and happy, but Jack didn't seem so happy.

"What's wrong?" I asked.

"Fucking Garry. I don't trust him."

"You don't trust anyone," I said. I was amused.

"You're too naïve. You trust everyone."

"I trust them until they give me reason to not trust them."

"That's your problem. We're dealing with criminals."

I remembered that Jack had done some time in jail. I learned later he'd been involved somehow in a murder, or attempted murder. I wish I'd known it sooner, and I probably wouldn't have agreed to have him as crew.

"As I said, I'll trust them until I have reason not to trust them. Plus, Ed's a successful businessman and hasn't ever been involved in anything like this. If he wants to keep doing it, it's in his best interest to keep all his promises."

"I still don't trust them. And I sure as hell don't trust Garry."

I'd realized that Jack had a rough past, but I hadn't seen this level of distrust yet. Garry told me later he didn't like Jack, either. The distrust was mutual. Garry told me that he knew Jack had done time even before getting to know him.

"I know the type," he told me. "I can smell jail on people. He reeked of it."

So, we'd done it again, and this time it had gone much more smoothly, like clockwork. I didn't know if that was because Ed was involved, or there were other reasons, but having a successful businessman doing the planning certainly seemed to make a difference. Having a plan to follow and knowing that things were set up in advance for us upon our return put my mind at ease throughout the operation. I hoped that if I did this again, Ed would once again be involved.

After a day or two of rest and relaxation in the marina, we prepared to return the boat to Miami and end the charter. The return date had been open-ended, which is why we paid so much extra. We did this so we wouldn't be on a timetable to get back to the marina on any specific date. Jack decided he was done, and would just wait for his money, so Greg and I, Maurice and Shannon—a couple whom I'd become close friends with—sailed the boat back north. We arrived at the marina in the early evening, and tied up in the slip. I left them on the boat and walked over to Garry's condo. He said he'd meet with the owners the next day and return the boat. He seemed happy and said everything was going well. He assured me I'd have my money within the week. As I was leaving, he handed me a gram of cocaine, uncut from a kilo package, and told me to share it with everyone on the boat. I said goodbye to Garry and Sarah and walked back to the boat.

We were tired, but hungry, and decided to get a bite to eat before going to sleep. I pulled out the cocaine and cut the entire gram into sixteen large lines. The four of us each did two large lines, half the gram. It was a stupid thing to do. Within a minute, we all knew we'd done too much. We felt our hearts racing, and we started to panic.

"Shit," I said. "What were we thinking?"

My friends Maurice and Shannon were both staring at me, blank expressions on their faces. I looked at Greg. His eyes were wide, and he took a deep breath.

"That probably wasn't a good idea," he said.

The effect was fast and powerful, and all we could do was sit and take deep breaths and try to calm ourselves, to talk our bodies down from the powerful rush of pure cocaine hitting our systems. It's a miracle we didn't die. We all sat for nearly half an hour, inhaling deeply and trying to will our bodies not to overreact to the drug. Looking back, I think the fact that we survived was because of the drug's purity. Had it been laced with speed or other popular cuts that cause an elevated heart rate, we might have died. We had no appetite by then. Food was the farthest thing from our minds. We only wanted to get through this alive. It was a sobering experience, and we all focused on one thing: survival. We sat in the cockpit of the sailboat the entire time, breathing deeply, willing our hearts to slow down.

Finally, after an hour, we realized that we were going to survive, but by then we were in no mood to party or eat and decided to call it a night. It was impossible to fall asleep right away, but within a few hours our bodies crashed as the cocaine wore off, and we slept soundly until morning, when we walked over to the bus station and caught the Trailways bus back to Key West.

Once back in town, I returned to my apartment, where I called Garry daily for progress reports on our money. He sounded vague and non-committal, and I grew worried that Jack may be right. Finally, after nearly two weeks, he said that Ed and Rick were coming down to the Keys to pay us. He gave me their number, and when I called, Ed answered the phone.

"Good news! I have most of the money, and we'll get down there and pay you guys."

He didn't go into any detail about what he meant by 'most of the money,' but I was just happy to hear that there'd be money coming our way. I rode my bike downtown and contacted Greg and Jack to let them know. Greg seemed relieved, but Jack never said a thing. I hadn't realized during the trip how much animosity he had toward Garry, but now that we were back, he wasn't making any attempt to hide it.

"He'd better pay us. He'd better pay us all of it, or he's going to hear from me," said Jack.

"What are you going to do? We can't fight him on it," I said.

"I have a gun. He'll hear from me."

That sort of talk worried me. Jack was being a tough guy, but you didn't wave a gun in Garry's face, because if you did, you'd be waving a gun in the face of the guy he worked for, Luis. And Luis was not a man you wanted to mess with. If you caused him trouble, he'd simply have one of his hitters take you out.

"You don't want to do that," I said.

"Just watch me," he replied.

"Let's not go there," said Susan, who was with him. "We're not getting into any gunplay. Right, Jack?"

He grunted something, and the problem seemed diffused for the moment. I was worried as well and wouldn't fully relax until the money, or any money, was in my hands, but I also knew that if the Miami people decided they weren't going to pay me, there was no recourse for me without putting my life at risk. It is what it is, I told myself. Trust them until they give you reason not to trust them. I was still comfortable that Ed would come through, so I just told myself to be patient.

Ed arrived in town and met with us at a popular outdoor restaurant. He was beaming and said everything was going well. They'd received almost all the money promised and were just waiting for a bit more. He handed $15,000 to both Jack and Greg, and I received $20,000, which was $10,000 shy of what I had been promised. Ed assured me I'd have the balance within another week or so, and at that point I had no reason to doubt him.

But three weeks passed, and I didn't hear from Ed. I pressed Garry on the matter and learned that he'd been furious that Ed had paid us personally, without giving the money to him first.

"You're *my* crew," he told me. "He has *no business* paying you directly."

When I heard this, I became worried, and with good cause. I was happy that Ed had paid me directly, because I was comfortable that Ed always told me the truth. When the rest of the money arrived, Ed contacted me and let me know that my $10,000 was with Garry. I contacted Garry, who grew angry that I'd spoken with Ed. Worse, I never got my last $10,000. Garry apparently just kept it, although he never told me this directly. He suggested that Ed hadn't given him all the money, so I had to decide which one I trusted. My worst fear had been realized, and now I was confronted with the reality that one of them had lied to me. Even though I got along well with Garry, I had to consider the fact that he'd just kept the money. I pressed the issue a few times, and his behavior and replies were vague enough that I had to come to terms with the fact that I wasn't going to get the last $10,000, and there wasn't anything I could do about it.

To make matters worse, my own use of drugs and alcohol was steadily increasing. I never saw it as a problem because I never drank or took drugs when I was feeling low. I drank and partied because I enjoyed it, I had the money for it, and it seemed to be what all my newfound friends expected from me. Without a real job, I became a regular at several local Key West bars, such as the Full Moon Saloon, Billie's, The Sandcastle, and The Half Shell Raw bar, where I'd worked before and been a bartender and manager.

I had access to lots of free coke through Garry, so I made it a point to always carry it on me while out and about, which made me a popular guy. In those days, it seemed to be an unwritten rule that if you had coke and a friend had coke, you always tried to do as much of theirs as you could before touching your own stash. I wasn't one of those guys. I shared with everyone. I was a man on a mission, and the mission was to have as much fun as I possibly could. I had so much fun that I'd often find myself lying awake late at night beside some woman I'd just met, drunk and coked out of my brains, wondering if I'd make it to thirty years in one piece. At that point, I'd bought into the "live fast, die young, and leave a beautiful corpse" philosophy.

With the money I'd made on the trip, I went on a shopping spree. It was the first time in my life I'd had access to that much money, and I was a kid in a candy store. My first purchase was a beautiful BMW R65 motorcycle, a classic "airhead" boxer twin bike like I'd always dreamed of getting someday. A car would have made more sense, but the bike was just too much to pass up. Next stop was the camera store. I'd always been a budding photographer with a love of images, so I purchased a brand-new Olympus OM-1 and a full set of top-shelf lenses for it. The last big-ticket item I purchased was a Cal 25 sailboat, a great little full cabin sailboat that would be ideal for living aboard, as well as sailing to the places I wanted to visit in the Caribbean and Bahamas. I was all set. I'd realized a dream, and I was proud of it.

I leased a slip for my new sailboat at Oceanside Marina. If I recall, it was about $125 a month for live-aboard fees, such as water, electric and cable TV. Right from the beginning, I loved my new life. I still had my apartment but also spent time living on a sailboat in a marina, driving a cool BMW motorcycle, had stacks of cash sitting in a safe deposit box in an Old Town bank, and everyone wanted to be my friend. I was Captain Kelly, a genuine pirate of Key West, and I enjoyed every minute of the experience.

I quickly discovered the downside of that lifestyle, however. It seemed that all those new "friends" were always asking me to loan them money. I often did and never got a dime back.

They'd also hit me up for coke and weed, which I supplied, and they never reciprocated. Up until that point in my life, I'd always been a trusting person, who'd give anyone the benefit of the doubt. Once I'd achieved my dream of being a drug-running sailor, having cash, access to drugs, and owning a boat, I quickly began to encounter the darker impulses of humanity. People I trusted and considered friends (even if casually) displayed their true colors over time. During the next few months, I found myself getting taken advantage of regularly, and rather than pulling the plug on them, I found myself avoiding them so I wouldn't have to say no to them. When you finally start feeling popular and the cool crowd starts paying attention to you, it's hard to say no to them. It was easier to just avoid them if I suspected they wanted something from me.

Overall, however, it was one of the most fun times of my young life to that point. I had everything I'd ever wanted in life and there was a deep sense of contentment most of the time. It was around then that I also began to think way too much about the cause and effect of my actions. I began to realize that by committing felonies, I was a criminal and a potential felon if caught. I had a difficult time with that realization but managed to push it from my head by thinking up ways to justify it. I knew that while my connection to the weed shipments was all fun and excitement, once it left the boat and started into the supply chain, there would be crimes, possibly even murders, attached to its distribution over time. I knew most of our shipments went to the northeast, in cities like Boston and New York, and that the Jamaican drug cartel was rapidly becoming violent as they fought for market share with Colombian cartels. Originally, the Jamaicans had just been front-end suppliers but realized there was way more money to be made at the back end of the business, at the street dealer level, and they wanted a share. Knowing that I was a player in this chain of crime bothered me, but not enough to make me want to stop.

I didn't have long to ponder it, though, as Garry soon began making plans for yet another trip. The past one had been so successful, and moved so smoothly, that he wanted to move quickly and try for a repeat. I asked if Ed and Rick would be involved.

"No," said Garry. "Who needs them? We know how to do it."

"But they're well organized and everything went smoothly with them. Why wouldn't we work with them again?"

"We don't need them," he said. "We know the blueprint. Let's just repeat it. Are you ready to go again? I'm ready. I'm getting another trip together, and we'll be ready in a few weeks."

"I'm in," I replied, but with concerns. "Can I still pick my own crew?"

Garry grinned his million-dollar salesman grin and slapped me on the shoulder. "Of course! You're Captain Kelly! You pick your crew. Always!"

I knew I didn't want Jack back on the boat, but I did want Greg again, so I asked him first.

"Hells yes!" he said. "When do we leave?"

That was easy. Now I had to find a second crew member.

I asked my friend Pete, who was a fishing buddy and fellow boat lover, if he'd be interested. Pete was a laid-back character who rarely had a bad word for anyone and even had a high tolerance when dealing with ass-holes. He was ex-Navy, had been to sea, and was a boat owner who loved the backcountry as much as I did. I was close friends with him and his girlfriend Barb and knew it would have to be a joint decision between the two of them. I got back to him after a few days to see how things had progressed.

"Can Barb come with me? Just on the way down, of course. She'll fly back from Jamaica once we get there."

"Of course. No problem there. I think Sarah's going again as well, so it'll look good arriving in port with women on board. Makes us look more like a bunch of friends on a cruise."

"Then we're in," he said with a grin.

And just like that, I had a crew and would be returning to Jamaica on a quick turnaround for another trip, hopefully just as quick and efficient as the last. If I'd had any idea how badly things would go, I don't think I would have gone. I know the lure of money and adventure was great, but I'd like to think I still had some sense of logic and reason working in my drug and alcohol-addled brain.

I contacted Garry and was shocked to learn he'd chartered the exact same boat for our next trip. I knew immediately that this was a dangerous move, as DEA agents roamed ports in the Caribbean and took photos of boats that raised suspicions, and I was certain that the boat we'd used the last trip had probably been photographed and ended up on a DEA list somewhere. After the women had flown back to the States on the last trip, Greg, Jack, and I were the only crew members on the boat, and it had to look suspicious when the women disappear, and suddenly there are just three single guys on a sailboat sitting around the Montego Bay Yacht Club drinking rum and waiting for a phone call. This bit of news gave me a bad feeling, but I didn't express it to Garry or my crew. I pushed it from my mind, telling myself once again 'It is what it is,' and moving forward with the decision.

From what I gathered talking to Garry, he'd spent a lot of time on the last trip getting to know our contacts in Jamaica and making friends and deals on his own while he was there. It became clear that Ed and Rick had just been a resource to be exploited, and once he met all their contacts, he didn't need them anymore. This trip would be run entirely by Garry, on direct approval from his boss, Luis. If we messed up, there'd be no buffer zone. Luis sat atop the food chain, and we ultimately answered to him. This also made me nervous, as Ed had brought a certain civility to the proceedings in our last trip, as well as being its major financier. That buffer zone was now removed.

The more I thought about the upcoming trip, the more concerned I became. We were going right back to the same ports, in the same boat. No consideration was given to mixing things up for our safety. I think it was around that point that I realized for the first time that we, the crew, were considered expendable resources. Yes, I was an experienced smuggling captain after two trips to two countries, but I was still expendable. The people running the show had multiple boats and crews doing the exact same thing that we were doing, but we never met them or knew anything about them. We might have even crossed paths at times, but because of the way Luis did business, most of the people working under him only knew a handful of people, and this separation of personnel was by design. The less we all knew, the less we could tell if caught. Being a businessman first and foremost, Luis must have had a certain amount of expected loss built into his operation, and played a game of percentages, and crews no doubt made up a large part of his loss margins.

Everything seemed so rushed as we prepared. In retrospect, it wasn't any more rushed than the last time, but my nerves were getting the best of me, and it made me feel rushed. I was aggravated by the lack of thought given to the operation. After working with Ed and Rick, I'd grown to like their style, which involved discussing every step with the crew so that we'd know exactly what to do and where to go at all times, as well as contingency plans if things went awry. This was in an era before cell phones, so we all used pagers and random pay phones. As the captain, I had a list of several pager numbers I could call when around a pay phone. I'd send the pay phone number to the pager and wait at the phone booth for a return call. It sounds like a slow and clumsy way to stay in contact, but when you're in the drug trade, it provides an untraceable way to stay in touch. We knew that the DEA—or any law enforcement officials—would have to have a just cause to bug a pay phone, so we used pay phones in residential neighborhoods, and near large, clean family shopping centers, where a phone tap would be highly unlikely.

We had the boat prepped and ready within a week, and we shuttled it down to Oceanside Marina, where I now lived almost full-time. I still kept my little apartment but didn't spend much time there. One of the advantages of living in the marina was getting to know all the locals who lived on their boats, as well as being able to see new boats and their crews coming and going. If there was a strange face wandering around, I was immediately aware of it. It was during this time that Vice President George H.W. Bush fronted the Southern Florida Drug Task Force focused on shutting down the Colombian cartel. The task force would be focused on two fronts: the money trail and the drug trail. It would be going after the bankers and money people, as well as the shipping and distribution side, which was my business.

In February of 1982, Vice President Bush announced, "Our investigative efforts will be as stringent on bankers and businessmen who profit from crime, as on the drug traffickers, the pushers, the hired assassins, and others. There will be no free lunch for the white-collar criminal." I wish I'd been paying closer attention to the news. It was now March of 1982, and I was getting a boat ready to sail down through the gauntlet of Coast Guard cutters and DEA aircraft that would be patrolling the Straits of Florida, and the Caribbean ports of known drug supplying countries would be infested with DEA agents. We were about to sail right into the thick of it. I didn't know all these details at the time, but I did have a very strong sense of fear and worry about this trip, and it only grew more pronounced by the day.

NINE

ROUND TWO

We got underway at last, setting sail for Grand Cayman Island, our first port of entry. I'd talked to Garry about allowing us to take it easy on the way down and have some fun along the way. Surprisingly, he agreed. I guess he figured a good crew was a happy crew. Me, Greg, Pete and his girlfriend Barb, Sarah (Garry's girlfriend, whom I liked a lot by now), and Johnny, a Key West local who had several friends with speedboats who'd be our unloading crew upon our return, were on board. In Jamaica, Barb, Sarah, and Johnny would all fly back to the States with Garry, and Greg, Pete, and I would repeat the exact same steps as my previous trip. We'd be back in Discovery Bay, wait for our signal, and pick up our load in the same place as last trip. The fact that virtually every step of the trip was a mirror image of the last one worried me greatly.

"But it's the best way," said Garry, who was a little exasperated with me. "It worked perfectly last time. Let's repeat that success."

"I don't like it. You're the one who taught me never to repeat anything in this business, as it's how you get caught. Repeating anything is lazy. Let's shake things up a bit, get a different pickup location, anything. This makes me nervous."

He just laughed at me and slapped me on the shoulder. "You're Captain Kelly. You'll be fine. Everything always works out for you. It'll work out this time, too."

I wasn't buying it. The feeling of dread was strong, but I kept it to myself.

We were underway at last and decided to make our first stop in the Dry Tortugas, a small archipelago about 70 miles west of Key West. It was just a few islands, but an interesting place because of the large Martello fortress on one of the islands. Fort Jefferson had been a prison for a while during and after the Civil War, and as noted earlier, had briefly held Doctor Samuel Mudd, the doctor who'd been imprisoned for his involvement in the Lincoln assassination. There was also a beautiful island to the west of it, Loggerhead Key, with a lighthouse and a long, deserted beach on its leeward side. After exploring the Fort, and snorkeling in the crystal-clear waters that surround it, we sailed over to Loggerhead Key and anchored. It was idyllic, and a welcome break (for me) from the mounting stress and dread I felt about this trip.

Cabin space was limited, and as the captain I always had first choice of the bunks, so I chose the forward bow cabin as usual, as it was the largest, most comfortable (when at anchor), and had its own head. Because I would only be sleeping in there about six hours a day, Sarah had once again taken to sharing it with me. She trusted me and seemed to feel comfortable sleeping beside me. I didn't get much sleep when she was in there with me, to be honest. I'd grown more attracted to her and having her lying beside me in a bikini was not a good recipe for a sound sleep, but I soldiered on.

We spent the day on the beach, lounging, reading books, swimming, snorkeling, and smoking weed. I would have been in heaven staying right there another week, doing the same thing every day, without worries, obligations, or any stress. But I knew we had to keep moving. We went back to the boat in the evening, watched the sunset, and got a good night's sleep. The following morning, I was up very early before dawn, pulled anchor and raised the sails myself, and set off for the western tip of Cuba.

The weather was perfect. The skies were clear, and a steady wind blew from the east, an ideal direction as we were heading southwest. We'd be fighting the current of the Gulfstream for the next day, so every knot of wind would be a blessing. The current was about 3 knots in that area, so if we were making 8 knots through the water, we were only gaining 5 over the bottom. Once around the tip of Cuba, we'd be out of the current, and tacking into the wind for a few days before arriving at Grand Cayman.

Just before nightfall the following day, we spotted the coast of Cuba. According to my calculations, we were about 15 miles offshore, a relatively safe distance, but I backed off a few miles once we sighted land. We saw small boat lights throughout the evening, and around midnight saw the lighthouse of Cabo San Antonio, the westernmost tip of Cuba. By early morning, we'd turned the corner and were officially in the Caribbean. I breathed a sigh of relief as we put Cuba in our rearview mirror and started our long port tack toward Grand Cayman. On the last trip, once around Cuba we'd taken a long port tack for over a day, then one long starboard tack north toward Cuba, and then one shorter port tack to approach the Cayman Islands. During the entire trip, this would be the least comfortable point of sail, as we'd be heading into the wind, and therefore the waves as well. Fortunately, we had a fair breeze, and small swells, so it wasn't terribly uncomfortable, although sleeping in the bow cabin meant you were rising and falling with the waves in a more pronounced manner, so I often catnapped in the center bunks, the pivot point of the boat, when I absolutely needed the sleep.

During the mid-morning of the second day since rounding the tip of Cuba, we heard a twin-engine aircraft. After a minute of looking into the sky ahead of us, we spotted it coming right toward us. I knew in my gut that this wasn't a passenger flight. Any passenger flight out of the Cayman Islands or Jamaica would have been a jetliner, and it wouldn't be flying the reverse of the course we were sailing. I called both the women on deck and had them sit in the cockpit as the twin engine aircraft, which looked like a Beechcraft King Air, flew over us about two thousand feet above the water. I thought it was going to keep going, but then it banked up sharply and turned around, and after dropping back down to its former elevation above the water, it came up on us from our stern. I knew for certain this was no commercial flight, and I was glad I'd pulled our inflatable dinghy up tight against the transom, partially blocking out the boat's name. As the aircraft flew over our heads, we all waved from the cockpit. It passed over us, banked into a steep turn ahead, and continued its way toward the western tip of Cuba. I shook my head.

"That wasn't any private aircraft, folks. I think we just had our picture taken by the DEA."

"What can they do? We haven't done anything yet," asked Sarah.

"They can't do anything right now. But you could bet if they got any information, or any photos with details, it'll go into some databank somewhere. You can bet someone will be wandering the docks in any port we stop, looking for boats and crews that match our description."

"We haven't done anything. They can't do anything to us."

"No, not yet. But if we're on a watch list, they'll be looking for us back in US ports within a few weeks. You can bet on that."

This revelation didn't seem to really bother anyone but me. Three of the crew, Sarah, Barb, and Johnny, would have nothing to worry about, as they wouldn't be anywhere near the boat when we were loaded and heading home. The only people who really had anything to worry about were me, Greg, and Pete, the smuggling crew. They didn't seem too worried, although Greg, who had a trip under his belt, did look at me a few times after the aircraft passed over us. I shrugged, he shrugged, and that was it. We didn't mention it again. I was under the belief that talking about bad luck could only manifest bad luck, so I just kept my mouth shut and tried to push the incident from my mind.

The remainder of the trip to Grand Cayman was uneventful, we were blessed with great weather, and we sailed into Georgetown harbor in midday. The water in the harbor was gorgeous and reminded me of Cozumel a year earlier. It was crystal clear for hundreds of feet, and the sailboat looked like it was floating on glass. We could see the keel of the boat from the dock, and while waiting for Customs to arrive, we put on our snorkels and jumped over the side for a swim and quick dive. Once we were cleared by Customs, we headed over to the King George Tavern and downed a few pints. It was nice to be back.

We'd already talked to Garry about spending a few days here and playing tourist, and he quickly agreed. He booked a room for himself and Sarah at a large resort up the coast, and we sailed up and anchored off the resort for the remainder of our stay. For the next few days, we played tourist. No stress, no worries, just a bunch of friends enjoying island life. We rented mopeds and toured the island, visited the turtle farms, ate lots of turtle, a huge dish in the Caymans, which is famous for turtle farms and turtle meat. Turtle meat was on every menu and seemed to be the major replacement for beef.

After two days, it was time to get back to work. We stocked up the boat and prepared to sail that evening. I was surprised to learn that Sarah would be back on the boat with us for trip from the Caymans to Jamaica. I had assumed she'd just fly to Jamaica with Garry, but he had plans to return to Miami first for some business, and then fly back to Montego Bay, where he'd meet up with us again. Sarah didn't seem happy with the arrangement, but I was happy she'd be joining us. I had grown comfortable sleeping beside her and enjoyed her friendship and small talk when we were in the bunk at the same time. I hadn't done anything to jeopardize our friendship, but it hadn't been easy restraining my feelings.

The weather forecast looked great, and it was clear sailing to Jamaica. The trip was going smoothly with no bad weather or holdups. I should have been happy, but the smoother things went, the more I worried. I could not escape the sense that we were going to get caught on this trip. I just knew it. When I started smuggling, a few friends had warned me to pay attention and trust my instincts, and if I felt anything was off or not right about a situation, then by all means get out of it if possible, and the sooner the better. Had I taken that advice to heart, I never would have signed on for the third trip, as I had a bad feeling from the beginning. At this point, I was too immersed in the trip to back out, and to do so would have carried some severe consequences. I hadn't forgotten who was backing this trip, and I didn't want to cross him by succumbing to last-minute cold feet.

It was on this leg of the trip that I finally ignored my better judgement and made a pass at Sarah. It wasn't really a sexual thing, but simply a move to be close to her, to hold her in my arms. We were in the bow cabin, and it was early evening. I wasn't on watch until midnight, and I was catching some rest. I was high, as usual, and might have had a few rum drinks under my belt. We'd just spent the past half hour chatting and laughing, enjoying each other's company, and then tried to get some sleep. I lay there, staring at her tanned back, and impulsively rolled toward her and put my arm over her, spooning gently against her back. It wasn't even a sexual move, or any attempt at sex. I simply felt comfortable with her and wanted to curl up and sleep with her in my arms.

Her reaction was violent. She exploded away from me, going from a drowsy sleep to wide awake in an instant. She spun around in the bunk and faced me sitting up.

"What are you doing? What are you doing?" She was trying to keep her voice down, but I'm sure the others heard it.

"Nothing. I was just trying to curl up with you. I wasn't making a pass at you."

"You can't do that! I'm with Garry! You know that!"

"I know. I said I wasn't making a pass at you. I just wanted to curl up, that's all."

"You can't do that! I'm with Garry," she said. She said it several more times just to make it clear that she was with Garry. I assumed she said it for anyone else who was listening in on us, in case her loyalty to Garry ever came into question.

Our eyes met, and I was surprised to see that she didn't look mad. She sounded mad, but her eyes said otherwise. I rolled away from her.

"Don't worry," I said. "It won't happen again."

"You know I'm with Garry. You can't do that."

"I know. I'm sorry. I wasn't hitting on you. Do you understand that?"

She smiled at me. In a whisper, she said, "I know. You just surprised me."

She lay down again, facing me. We talked some more and finally fell asleep. I drifted off realizing that she wasn't mad and even seemed amused that I'd made a pass at her, even though nothing could ever come of it. The next day, instead of any awkwardness between us, we seemed to be even better friends, and life quickly returned to normal.

We arrived in Montego Bay about a day later and once again tied up at the Montego Bay Yacht Club, in the same slip we'd tied up in on our last trip. I really hadn't given much thought to the fact that we'd never cleared Customs when leaving on our last trip, so I was caught off guard when the Customs official began grilling me in an aggressive manner. It took me awhile to realize where his questioning was leading, but it became evident that he felt he had to do something. As I described this story at the start of the book, I won't get into as much detail this time around, but after satisfying his demands, and giving him a large bribe, we were in the clear—at least for the moment. Garry was always optimistic and told me to put it behind me. I was a worrier and couldn't, and it only added to the sense of dread I was feeling on this trip. I'm still not certain it was just dread

I was feeling, and I suspect it was dread mixed with a sense of guilt over what I was doing. I was still struggling with the fact that I was committing felonies, and it conflicted with my view of myself as one of the good guys. I was a criminal, in the act of committing crimes, and yet finding time to enjoy myself while I justified what I was doing. It was a complex situation to have rolling around in my mind, especially at that age and with little life experience to call upon. There were moments where I even found myself wishing to get caught, so I'd have an excuse to stop. I was hooked on the adrenaline, money and lifestyle, and I knew I would keep doing it until I got caught. It was only natural to allow a certain part of my mind to allow that thought to come into play.

We decided to spend a few days playing tourist in Montego Bay, and I was glad to have another break to take my mind off the sense of doom I was feeling. Within a day after arriving, I found myself enamored with a beautiful woman named Lauren from Boston, who was hanging out in Jamaica and spent a lot of time at the Yacht Club. She was a natural beauty with black hair, light skin, and gorgeous green eyes that sparkled when we talked. I was instantly smitten and found myself heading into the bar any time I'd see her there. In a short few days, we became friends and chatted every time we crossed paths. She was very bright and savvy about life and clearly had no intention of hooking up with a smuggling boat captain. From our conversation and her questioning, I knew that she knew exactly who I was and what I was up to, and while she enjoyed hanging out with me, she wasn't the type who'd go for a one-night stand. However, she did give me her contact information in Boston and told me to look her up if I ever made it Boston. She made it clear that she liked me and enjoyed my company but would not consider anything else until I was back in the States and involved in something with a better future than being a smuggler. I saved her information, and three years later, on a trip to Boston, tried to contact her. But that's another story for another time.

The idyllic life at the yacht club was about over. We'd gone to Jamaica to conduct business, and now it was time to do business. During the few days we'd been at the yacht club, there'd been two guys wandering the docks. They were American, and I was certain they were DEA agents. Both were dressed in brand new deck shoes with khaki shorts and tropical print shirts that still had new creases on them, as if they'd come right off the shelf. I watched them at the bar, and they spent most of their time watching boats come and go. They'd walked the dock while we were all on the boat, and I'd nodded to them and said hello. They acted a bit odd, which only confirmed my suspicion that they were from some American law enforcement agency.

Normally, the first questions you'd be asked by other sailors were where you'd come from, what port was next on your itinerary, which boat you were on, and so forth. This was a standard greeting talk among sailors. These guys avoided asking any questions, which added to my suspicions. I was surprised to realize that these guys were not masters of disguise, but quite clumsy and obvious. In their attempts to blend in, they only made themselves stand out more than ever. We started referring to them as Tweedle Dee and Tweedle Dum, and they were still hanging around the marina several days later when we set off for Discovery Bay to make our pickup.

In our days before the pickup, we rented a car and took a day trip down to Negril. It was a beautiful drive. Garry and Sarah stayed behind, so it was just me, Greg, Pete, Barb and Johnny. Negril was a blast, filled with Americans, and after a day of swimming, smoking weed on the sea cliffs and eating a spice cake so full of high-quality weed that I almost forgot my name, we drove back to Montego Bay and crashed on the boat too beat to even make dinner. The next day we shopped and stocked up the boat for the return trip. We planned to leave the harbor at first light to avoid being seen by the suspected DEA agents, who we assumed were sleeping off a hangover at some resort, courtesy of the American taxpayers.

With the vacationing out of the way, it was time to get down to business. We paid our tab at the Yacht Club the evening before our departure, I said goodbye to Lauren with the hope of seeing her again someday, and we got a good night's sleep. The women stayed on the boat until late, just in case anyone was watching us, and around midnight they left and went to a hotel.

They'd get a good night's sleep and fly back to the States the next day. We slipped out of our berth at the crack of dawn the next morning, sailed through beautiful Montego Bay, and out into the Caribbean, right into a brisk headwind. We'd been running with our large jib since leaving the marina, but once we were through the sheltered bay and had turned the corner past Dead End Beach, we caught the full brunt of the swells and strong breeze. While dropping the large jib to raise the smaller one—which would be better suited for the heavier headwinds—the guys lost control of the large jib and it was pulled into the sea. They tried to pull it out, but once it was more than half submerged, it was gone. They simply couldn't summon the strength to pull it back on deck, and it was in danger of getting tangled in the rudder assembly. I hated to do it, but I told them to just cut it loose and let it go. We couldn't endanger the boat or the job over a sail, and I figured it would be cheaper to replace than to risk recovering, so they cut it loose. It was an eerie sight watching that large white sail sink away into the deep below us, slowly turning turquoise, and then disappearing into the depths.

With the small jib up, we were sailing very efficiently and would be at Discovery Bay with plenty of time to relax and see the community on shore. The guys wanted to go ashore again, but at that point, I'd had enough of the tourism and just wanted to focus on the task at hand. It was another perfect day in Paradise, and the cruise up the coast was exhilarating. There was enough wind and swell to make it interesting, and all three of us stayed in the cockpit for the entire trip, as it was too rough to go below and relax or sleep. By late afternoon we'd reached Discovery Bay. Garry hadn't given us a confirmation of the time, and all we knew for certain was to anchor in the same spot as last time and wait for our signal from shore. If we didn't get a signal, we just waited another night. I had no problem with that, although I would have preferred to have everything planned out as tightly as the last trip with Ed and Rick.

I had the impression that we were running by the seat of our pants once again, just like the Mexico trip, where nothing was set in stone and everything seemed to happen spur of the moment, on a whim. I hated the uncertainty but had grown use to Garry's way of operating. He liked to keep everyone guessing right up until the last moment. His philosophy was simple. Plans could be discovered, so don't share plans with anyone. Just do what you need to do when you need to do it. It was frustrating for everyone working with him, but I understood the purpose behind the intentional disorder.

Having spent so much time on ocean-going sailboats in the past year, I was getting very good at sailing in tight quarters rather than using the motor. We sailed into the bay, picked out our anchorage, and sailed right to the spot under the small jib alone. Once in position, I turned dead into the wind, luffed the jib, and Greg dropped anchor. Now the clock was ticking. Would it be tonight? I hoped so. I would have enjoyed another day or two on the island, but I also just wanted to get back and get it over with. Despite all the fun we'd had, I really hadn't been able to enjoy myself. I just wanted it to be over. If this trip was to end badly, I wanted it to happen as fast as it could.

After not getting all my money on the last trip, and with Ed and Rick out of the game, I worried about getting paid for this trip, should it go well. While enjoying ourselves on the island in the previous days, I'd briefly met with Garry and two of the Jamaican gang members who were working with us. Garry introduced them as important people in the group, so I spent some time talking to them. I asked if they'd be the ones prepping the load and delivering it to the boat. One of the men stepped forward.

"I be on the boat. I be there."

I shook his hand and started to chat with him. We were at a location up in the hills, and I mentioned to him that I'd like to get my hands on some top-quality sinsemilla, the best he had. He mentioned that he sold a very high-grade sinsemilla and took me to a truck to show it to me. From behind the seat, he pulled large flat package that was the size of a couch cushion, about 24 inches square, and tightly packed. I held it and tossed it up in the air. It felt like a nice amount.

"What's it weigh?" I asked him.

"Twenty pound."

"How much?"

"Five hundred."

I was shocked. Five hundred dollars for a 20-pound slab of high-quality, gummy, sticky sinsemilla was dirt cheap. Even in bulk form, this would go for many thousands of dollars back in the States.

I reached for my wallet, but he shook his head.

"No, not now. I bring it on the boat. Have my money then. I deliver; you pay me then."

I was relieved and thanked him profusely. All I could think about was handing over $500 and never seeing it again. As we were leaving, Garry nodded toward the guy and then looked at me.

"Side deal?"

"Just getting in on the action a bit. I wanted to get some high-grade stuff for personal use."

He burst out laughing. "Twenty pounds isn't personal use. But I hear you. No problem from my end, as long as your personal dealings don't interfere with the main shipment."

As we drove away, I felt a strong sense of relief, bolstered by Garry's approval of my actions. I had some insurance, some guarantee that if I could get through this without getting busted, at the very least I had some product I could sell to provide some income. That twenty pound block, broken down into quarter ounces and ounce bags, could easily bring me about twenty times what I paid for it. Looking back, it was a good decision. Always get the insurance. Always provide a way to cover your bills if the main gig falls apart. I was learning quickly.

It was a lazy, relaxed evening on the boat. Although we hadn't planned to go ashore, I changed my mind and decided it wouldn't hurt to take a nice break while we waited. We paddled ashore for about half an hour and visited a local store to buy some soda and cigarettes. None of us were really smokers, but we liked to smoke while sailing. There was something very calming about the salty breeze, the sun, and the rush of smoke hitting your lungs. Since we were throwing caution to the wind at every turn, taking up smoking for a few months just seemed par for the course. Plus, it was fun smoking foreign cigarettes, and Jamaica's favorite brand, Craven A, made us feel exotic and mysterious. We sat down by the harbor drinking our sodas and smoking cigarettes. From my right, a young attractive local woman approached me. She looked tentative but smiled a lot as she approached. She walked up to me.

"Are you the captain?"

"Yes," I replied.

"I'm Yvonne. May I speak with you in private?"

My first thought was that I was being lured away to get robbed, and I must have shown it, because she quickly waved her hands in front of her.

"No, no, no. You don't have to go anywhere. I just need to talk to you."

I still wasn't sure and looked around. We were at the edge of a small park, near the water.

It was an open area, and I didn't see anyone else around. I decided she was safe, so I walked toward her.

"Be back in a minute, guys," I said to Greg and Pete.

"No worries."

I walked with Yvonne toward the water's edge, making sure we were in plain sight of Greg and Pete.

"What can I do for you?"

"I want to go back with you. I want to go to Miami."

I was caught off guard. "I can't do that. It's not legal."

"Please," she said. She grabbed my arm softly with both hands and looked me square in the eyes. "I will do anything. I will do anything, anything." She held my gaze so that I'd know exactly what she was talking about when she said "anything."

I ran all the possible scenarios through my head, and for a split second I was tempted to say yes, but with the understanding that she wouldn't have to do anything. The last thing I wanted to do was take advantage of someone desperate to get to a better life. I also knew that Garry would flip out if he discovered what I'd done without his permission, even though he was about to pull something on me that I wasn't prepared for.

I held her hands and told her I was sorry, but there wasn't anything I could do.

"Please," she repeated. "I will do anything at all you ask."

"I'm sorry, but I'm just not able to take you. We don't have enough food, and there probably wouldn't be room on the boat."

"I know what you're here for. I don't need to eat much. I can bring some food if you say yes."

"You don't understand, Yvonne. I just can't. I work for people, and they would not agree to it. I might get in trouble."

She looked distressed, like she might cry. I felt terrible but knew we simply could not take a passenger. I was already smuggling weed. The last thing I needed if caught was a human trafficking charge on my record.

"Do you have family in Miami?" I asked.

I knew this was increasingly common with the explosion of the Jamaican weed trade. Many of the local gang members moved to Miami to put themselves in a better position to conduct business and eliminate middlemen, much to the chagrin of the Colombians who were then running nearly everything. It was increasingly common to get one family member into Miami, where they'd set up a household, and bring over more family members. Nearly all were affiliated with the gangs and worked for them in some manner. I suspected Yvonne was related to—or closely affiliated—with some Jamaican gang member already living in the States.

"Yes," she said. "I have a place to go when I get there. I wouldn't be a problem."

"No, I can't take you. Maybe I can get word to someone for you?"

She looked amused. "I can use the telephone for that, thank you."

I looked at her for a while. She seemed like a sweet and lovely person, but there was simply no way in Hell I was going to smuggle a Jamaican back to the States, especially one possibly tied to a gang.

She looked crestfallen as we left. I had thought that most of it was an act, but she appeared genuinely distraught and sat on the shore for over an hour after we'd paddled back out to the sailboat. I sat in the cockpit smoking a cigarette, and right around dark she stood up and walked down the dark street near the park, slowly disappearing into the night.

We began to watch the shore for our signal. There was a small parking lot near the seaside park, and whoever had signaled us on the last trip had done so from there. We watched it again, but I had Greg and Pete keep a wide view of shore, just in case they signaled from elsewhere. About an hour after dark, we all three saw the three blinks from a green light. After a short pause, three more, and after another short pause, three more. They would keep blinking until we flashed our running lights at them. I had Greg go below and turn the running lights on and off three times, our signal that we'd seen their signal. I started up the engine, and we pulled anchor and motored out of the harbor. In about an hour, the boat would have a ton of prime Jamaican weed packed below decks, and we'd be on our way back to the Keys. As I steered the boat out of the harbor, I remember promising myself that if this trip went as planned and we didn't get busted, I was going to quit. Win, lose or draw, I was done. I had what wanted out of it—a sailboat, a motorcycle, an interesting reputation, and a nice chunk of cash—and now it was time to move on while I was still alive to enjoy the fruits of my labor.

We motored out of the harbor and anchored just beyond the natural reef barrier that protected the harbor, as close as possible to the place where we'd picked up our load on the last trip. The sense of dread was still with me, but I'd grown use to it and resigned myself to whatever fate might await me. Soon the Jamaicans came out with their skiffs, and we got the boat loaded quickly, as we were getting good at this. This was my third trip, and I considered myself a professional. Suddenly, without warning, one of the Jamaican gang members climbed into the cockpit and sat down. As mentioned earlier, at the start of this story, we learned his name was Muggy, and that we were to deliver him to the United States. This was the first I'd heard of this development. Garry could have told me, but he didn't, and I suspect that's why he didn't complain when he saw me cutting my own weed deal with one of the gang members. I believe that he let it slide because he knew he'd be catching me off guard when I found out I was also smuggling a Jamaican gang member into the USA. I was also very relieved that I'd refused Yvonne's request earlier. That last thing I needed was two illegal and unexpected passengers.

By this point in the trip, I'd surrendered any belief that I was in control of my destiny. By now, I felt I was trapped in a strong current, and it was carrying me somewhere, and I had no control over where it would take me. I'd given myself over to this feeling, which was not a good place for someone who's supposed to oversee sailing a ton of weed and a Jamaican gang member back into America without getting caught. I looked at my large purchase and was glad that I'd made the decision to buy it. I told myself that no matter what happened, I would get that package into a safe place as quickly as possible upon our return, because I felt I was going to need it.

With our load secured, and Muggy below deck, we set sail for the Yucatan channel. This stretch of sailing was probably my favorite on the entire trip. We were still safe while sailing in the Caribbean, and we'd have several days running downwind, surfing the waves, and generally getting used to being at sea for a non-stop voyage back to the Keys. The trips down were fun, with stops for pleasure, but the return trip was all business with a single goal in mind: run the gauntlet of Coast Guard cutters and DEA aircraft and arrive safely back in the Keys with the load. That was my single goal right now, and my third trip, and I was confident in my ability to pull it off.

During the two days following our departure from Jamaica, Muggy never came above deck. He lay on his bunk and slept. We offered him food several times, but he shook his head. He wasn't particularly talkative and only communicated when it was necessary. I suspected he'd never been at sea for any length of time and was just experiencing seasickness as his body adjusted to the constant rolling and pitching experienced on an oceangoing sailboat. I had always felt that people got seasick because they tensed up their body and tried to counteract the rolling and pitching, when the secret was to just let your body roll with the motion. It was the resistance that triggered the seasickness.

For the entire run to the Yucatan Channel, we had perfect weather. Soft, puffy clouds, lots of sunshine, and a steady, even breeze that barely changed directions. It was easy sailing, and we had the spinnaker pole holding the jib out, sailing "wing on wing," as it's called. This was the most relaxing way to sail for any length of time, and we quickly fell into our routines.

We finally reached the western end of the Caribbean and turned north into the Yucatan Channel, well below Cozumel. We'd stay in international waters, but we'd be able to see land for some time before moving up into the Gulf of Mexico. After our course change, we had the wind on our starboard beam, and the boat was making excellent time, as we were making about eight knots through the water, and with the three knots of the Gulfstream added in, we averaged around eleven knots per hour over the bottom, a great pace for an overloaded sailboat.

I had brought an old guitar on this trip and played it often. It was how I relaxed. I'd sit up on the deck in front of the mast, strum, pick, and sing a bit, and it helped me calm my anxieties. While sailing up the coast that morning, I had the guitar in the cockpit and started singing Bob Marley's "Three Little Birds."

It's a beautiful, simple melody with equally simple lyrics, but it's one of those songs that usually brought a pause in the conversation when played around campfires or a backyard. It was the 1980s, and Bob Marley was a huge star, especially in Florida and the Caribbean. He'd passed away just a year earlier, and the love of his music had grown tremendously. I strummed and sang in the cockpit, while Greg had the helm. Suddenly, I saw Muggy pop his head up through the hatch and make eye contact with me. His eyes were very bloodshot, and he looked high and tired, like he'd woken up from a bender a bit too soon.

He had a small smile on his face.

"Good morning," he said. "How are you today?"

This was the most he'd spoken directly to us since coming aboard. "We're doing great," I replied. "How are you?"

"Getting adjusted. I not sail like dis before."

"I didn't think so. Not many people have. Come on up and have a seat. It's nicer up here than down below. The fresh air will be good for you."

Muggy climbed into the cockpit and sat across from me. He motioned for me to keep playing, so I did. When I was done, he had a big smile on his face.

"Ah, Bob" he said. "Bob the best."

"I know a lot of his songs," I replied.

"Ah, then sing them!"

And I did. Throughout the morning, over strong coffee and a few joints, I played every Bob Marley song I knew. It was a glorious morning. The sun was shining, music filled the air, and after Pete joined us in the cockpit and cooked breakfast for everyone, the mood was ebullient. We laughed, talked, and learned about Muggy, who'd gone from silent and untrusting, to very open and friendly with us. I had to keep reminding myself that he was an enforcer, and that he was on the boat to protect the shipment at all costs, and if we were deemed a threat, he would deal with us. I reminded myself of this, but couldn't help but think we'd won him over, and that he (somewhat) trusted us.

Muggy was a fascinating character. He was not dressed like an islander, but more like a New York street hustler. His clothing choices were reminiscent of the character Huggy Bear from the popular Starsky & Hutch TV show, which had been very popular in the late 1970s. He wore a fuzzy derby with a small brim, a purple sweater with a half-zipper and a giant ring to pull it, thick wool-like purple plaid pants, and high-top, zip-up hipster boots. He'd been dressed this way since coming aboard, and we'd wondered if he had a change of clothes with him. It was going to be difficult getting him off the boat in Florida without being noticed unless we could talk him into changing into something a bit less conspicuous, and a bit less smelly. He'd clearly been wearing this outfit for more than a few days, and it smelled like it.

We learned that he had some relatives in Miami, and once the shipment was secured and out of our hands, he'd join them. He seemed to be a decent guy, and I suspected that we were seeing a bit of his true character away from the daily demands of being part of a drug gang in Jamaica, where his personality was different out of necessity. He'd come aboard with a very small rucksack, which he'd used for a pillow while sleeping. I could see the butt of a semi-automatic pistol inside the rucksack, but he never took it out in our presence. I knew that we had nothing to worry about. We all had the same goal, and that was to make certain the shipment made it safely to the next drop-point, at which time it would be someone else's responsibility.

Over the next few days, as we sailed north and into the Gulf of Mexico, we all became friends with Muggy. I could tell he genuinely liked our company, and once that initial barrier had been broken down, he became a genial, friendly and interesting member of the crew. After a few days of interaction, he trusted us enough to share a few things with us. He'd brought a bottle of some very dark brown liquid with him, and we'd been wondering what it was, and why he seemed to guard it so carefully. He also pulled a small stash of weed from his backpack and came up on deck with the bottle. He rolled a blunt and lit it, then passed it to his right, to Pete.

"Lamb's Breath," he said. "The breath of the Lamb." He said it reverently, as if we all knew the importance of his words. We didn't but quickly realized it meant something to him.

"What is Lamb's Breath?" I asked.

"The finest. It's the best we grow. A special plant."

Well, he didn't have to tell me twice. I took it next and drew hard on it. The flavor was incredible, and I could see the tar and resins collecting on the inside of the paper as I pulled on the joint. Within a few minutes, I could tell it was special. I could barely focus for more than a few seconds.

"So, you work on the distribution end of the business?" I asked him.

"No, I'm one of the growers. I love to grow things."

"So can you identify your own products?" I asked.

"Yes, I know all my work. A grower must be like a man who makes wine, who knows his grapes, and can tell you everything about his wine. I am like that."

This was intriguing. Muggy was an enforcer and shipment guardian but clearly wasn't a hardcore gang member. Learning that he was a grower explained a lot about his personality, and now I was seeing him for what he was, and how he saw himself . . . as an artist.

"So, if I show you something I purchased from your organization, you could identify it?"

"Yes, mon. I know my own work."

I went below and grabbed my 20-pound pack of weed. Taking a knife from the galley, I carefully cut into one of the corners. I extracted a large, gummy bud from the package, and took it back on deck. I handed it to Muggy.

He smiled. "Lamb's Breath. This is Lamb's Breath. The best. Same as what we smoked."

I had to sit down. I was overjoyed. I'd purchased twenty pounds of Jamaica's finest for just five hundred dollars.

"I'm curious. Why would your guy give me your best product?"

He didn't hesitate. "He think you may be back again. He want you to come to him first. He think everyone a future customer, so he treat you right."

I took my pack of weed below and carefully sealed it up. I was going to protect this with my life. The amount of money I could make from this would be way more than I'd previously thought. My insurance payout just went up by a large margin. I went back on deck, and Muggy was opening the bottle of dark brown liquid.

I nodded at it. "What's that?"

He laughed. "My magic rum," he said. "Try some."

He handed me the bottle, and I took several large swigs without knowing what I was getting into. I could immediately tell it was laced with marijuana of some sort. I held it at arm's length while I coughed.

"What the hell is this?"

He laughed again. "It's my magic rum. Appleton's with pressed sinsemilla juice. I squeeze the resin from buds and add it to the rum."

Fuck me. I'd just taken a huge swig and probably ingested way more THC than I'd ever done in my life. I spent the rest of the afternoon on deck, staring at the sky, talking to the clouds, humming Bob Marley songs, working on my tan, telling myself I was Captain Kelly, and every little thing was gonna be all right.

After a few more days, we were well up into the Gulf of Mexico and we were starting to see more freighters coming and going into the Gulf from the Straits of Florida. The DEA and other agencies involved in Bush's Southern Florida Drug Task Force were focusing their efforts on the Straits, and the waters to the south of the Keys. At that point, we were northwest of the Keys, and approaching from that direction, which would not attract any attention, as the area was also filled with fishing vessels and other sailboats coming down the west coast of Florida. This plan had worked perfectly on the last two trips, so it was only natural to go back to the well one more time.

While at sea, I hadn't dealt with any of the dread I'd been feeling. I only seemed to feel that way around land and other people. At sea, I was a free man. More importantly, my mind was free and clear, and I could enjoy the moment to the fullest. I loved living in the moment, where nothing else mattered other than that which was right there with me, at that moment in time. Being at sea allowed a mental freedom I've never experienced anywhere else in my life. You simply don't have access to the things that drag you down in daily life. No obligations, no phone calls, no appointments, no responsibilities other than the task before you, which is to keep the boat on course and moving forward. I imagine it must be similar to being in space, looking down on your world and your life, and feeling you're somehow outside of it all, looking back in. Being at sea provides a unique separation from your routines, and it greatly simplifies your life, breaking it down to its most basic elements. At sea, although we were all captive on a small space twenty-four hours a day, we managed to create our own separate worlds to live in, our own head space, and it was a beautiful thing, and difficult to describe to someone who's never experienced it.

As we approached land, I began to worry again. I was vaguely aware of the Task Force presence in the Keys but had pushed it from my mind. I knew we'd have to be particularly careful once we made landfall, and that there would be eyes everywhere watching any boat activity. I didn't want to draw attention, so I talked with the guys about my plan for getting the boat safely to our unloading site. The DEA, Customs agents and Marine Patrol would be checking out any suspicious boating activity in the small islands north of the Keys, known to locals as 'the backcountry,' so going there was out of the question. Considering how strongly the boat smelled of weed, I didn't want to risk pulling into a marina like we had after the Mexico trip. I decided that I'd do exactly what I'd done on the last trip. We'd sail right up to the anchorage at the Casa Marina resort, drop anchor, and go ashore like we owned the place. They wouldn't be expecting it, and once again, it seemed like the best way to hide a boat filled with weed was to hide it in plain sight, right under their noses.

That was my decision, and the guys agreed with it. It had worked before, and made the most sense now, as any attempt to hide a large sailboat out in the backcountry would immediately draw suspicion when spotted. Once again, we sailed south into the channel between the Dry Tortugas and the Marquesas Keys, took a left turn, and sailed toward Key West. We arrived early morning, dropped sail about half a mile from the resort, and motored to our anchorage. We made sure we were freshly shaved and dressed in spiffy yachting clothes rather than our usual dirtbag collection of baggy swimsuits and tee-shirts, and we made certain Muggy stayed below. A tall black man dressed in furry purple clothing would look very out of place on the boat and immediately draw attention to us. After dropping anchor, we all went below and watched the shore through binoculars. We scanned the patio, where breakfast was being served, and saw nothing suspicious. Virtually everyone looked like a tourist, intent on enjoying their vacation at Key West's most classic resort.

The decision was made to go ashore and check things out. We'd walk around the resort, get a feel for the vibe, and see if there was anyone suspicious lurking around. I volunteered to go first and had Greg row me ashore. Before I left the boat, I took my 20-pound package of Lamb's Breath, folded it gently, and stuffed it into my waterproof duffle, zipped it shut, and then sprayed down the outside with Lysol. After a minute, I wiped it clean. It seemed to hide the smell, so I boarded the dinghy, and Greg paddled me to shore. I jumped out on the beach, waved goodbye, and walked through the guests having breakfast on the patio, and right into the main lobby.

Without getting too close to the check-in desk, I made my way through the lobby, out the front door, and walked to my apartment, which was less than a quarter mile from the resort.

It felt wonderful to be home, to be safe, if only for a few hours. I took my duffel bag out into the back yard, climbed up into the large banyan tree, and hid the bag about fifteen feet off the ground, well out of sight of anyone in my yard. With that task done, I felt a sense of accomplishment. No matter what happened from that point forward, I'd have something to fall back on, to cover my ass. And if everything went well and according to plan, it would just be a bonus. After stashing the bag, I went into my apartment, opened all the doors to air it out, and took my first real shower in two weeks. It was glorious. I stood under the scalding water until the tank ran dry, then toweled off and laid down for a bit. I felt guilty knowing the guys were still on the boat, so I cleaned up, got dressed, and walked back to the resort.

On the way I called Garry's pager and waited for his reply on a corner payphone near the end of Truman Avenue. I let him know where we were, and he let me know he was already in town and staying at a local motel out near the bridge to Stock Island. When I returned to the Casa Marina, I walked out onto the back patio and was surprised to find Greg and Pete eating breakfast and drinking mimosas. When they saw me, they both grinned. I would have preferred that they'd stayed on the boat, but I understood their need to get off, so I said nothing. I sat down and joined them, ordering my own brunch as soon as I could.

"Well, we did it again," said Greg.

"Not yet. We're not out of the woods yet."

"Pretty close, though. I thought it would be easier to watch the boat from here. That's why we came ashore."

"No problem," I said. "I get it. How's Muggy doing?"

"He wanted to come ashore, too. I told him I'd bring him some breakfast."

"I feel bad leaving him out there alone while we're in here enjoying a great breakfast."

"I am going to take him a full plate in a bit. He'll be okay," said Greg.

I casually glanced around the patio while we talked. Still nothing suspicious. Nobody was paying any attention to the boat. I walked down to the shore to check if there was any smell from the boat. Fortunately, the breeze was not blowing onshore, so any strong smells would be blown farther down the shoreline, hopefully dissipating and preventing anyone from tracing it to its source. I motioned for Greg and Pete. They picked up the spare breakfast on a paper platter, and we rowed back out to the boat. I still hadn't decided what to do with Muggy, but once on the boat, watching him devour the fresh breakfast, I made my decision.

"Muggy, when you're done with breakfast, I'm going to give you some of my clothes. We're going to take you ashore and get you on the bus to Miami. I spoke to Garry, and we'll probably be unloading tonight. You'll be in Miami before the shipment arrives. How does that sound to you?"

He nodded. "It sounds good to me."

"Any questions or concerns?"

"No," he said. "None. I'm fine."

After he was done with the breakfast, I told him to take a shower and get scrubbed up. I told him the weed smell was on everything (which it was), but he was also ripe himself after two weeks without a bath. The head on the boat had a small shower, but no hot water, so most of us used it to just rinse salt off our bodies. I told Muggy to scrub hard and take as long as he needed.

I handed him a pair of loose khaki dungarees and a worn t-shirt from a Key West bar, and a Heineken ball cap. I tried to dress him like a sailor, to help him fit in. He put on the clothes and didn't look anywhere near as conspicuous as he had before. I had him put his old smelly clothes into a garbage bag and seal it up to hide the smell. I instructed him to just act natural and relaxed and be calm until we got him safely through the hotel.

I paddled him ashore and made sure I kept him talking and smiling as we paddled, just in case we were being watched. After hitting the beach, I decided to take him around the outside of the building rather than through the lobby. We walked through a security gate together, around to the front of the resort, and I paid a cab driver to take him to the bus stop. We shook hands, I thanked him for his company on the trip, and I never saw him again. Garry told me later that he'd made it safely to Miami, and all had gone well at his end. I later tried to look him up through Garry's Jamaican contact in Miami but was informed Muggy had returned to Jamaica.

I returned to the boat, and we talked about our plan of action for the next 24 hours. We were very, very close to being safe, and we didn't want to mess it up. We decided that we'd lock up the boat, get away from it, and not return until it was time to go offshore and unload it. It was safe to leave the boat there without any complaints from the Casa Marina staff. They only owned the land right up to the shoreline and couldn't tell us not to anchor in front of the resort. If they'd wanted to, they might have told us we couldn't land our dinghy on their beach, but at that time, the resort was quite okay with locals hanging out in the clubs, bars, and restaurants in the resort, and didn't care when locals came for the day just to use the beach, as long as they ordered food and drinks from the bar.

With a great sense of relief, we walked through the resort, out the front door, and all three of us piled into a cab, which dropped us off at our homes. We agreed to touch base a few hours before sunset, and I told them I'd talk with Garry to find out when we'd unload.

I was the last out of the cab, and I paid the driver and walked slowly to my apartment's front door. I was suddenly overcome with a deep exhaustion and realized I was simply relaxing both my body and mind for the first time in many weeks. By the time I got to my front door, I was already nodding off. I opened the door, tossed my small bag on a chair, set an alarm clock, and fell onto the couch, where I slept soundly until my alarm went off at 4 P.M.

I woke up feeling refreshed, but still not comfortable. I paged Garry from a pay phone across the street from my house on Margaret Street, right in front of the Cuban eatery where I loved to get breakfast and a Cuban coffee almost every morning. He called me back within a minute and told me everything was on for that evening.

"Good," I said. "I'm ready to hand this one off to someone else."

"Be careful. I've been here a week. This town is absolutely crawling with Feds. They're everywhere."

"What's going on? Why the huge presence?"

"Lots of shipments coming in, I guess. I think they're looking for bigger fish than you, but don't drop your guard."

I knew that the Coast Guard liked to focus on larger freighter ships because they carried more, but I also knew that they'd bust any boat, regardless of cargo size. We wouldn't be safe until the boat was empty and cleaned up.

"Just do the usual. Johnny's guys are already watching you and know where you're at."

He didn't need to go into any detail. We'd already discussed this part with Johnny on the way down to Jamaica. Once Garry alerted him that we'd returned, he and his buddies watched the boat. There was so much small boat traffic along the Atlantic shore of the island that they'd just be lost in the crowd. It was reassuring to know they'd already been watching us, and all we'd have to do is get about a mile offshore, somewhere between the Casa Marina and Stock Island, and they'd come right to us.

From the pay phone, I called Pete and Greg and let them know to meet me back at the Casa Marina beach by seven that evening. Once I'd contacted them, I set my alarm and took another nap. Almost home, and hopefully by this time the next day, I'd be resting easy and waiting for my money. And then I'd be done, ready to start enjoying life as a hardworking civilian.

My alarm went off. I woke up, dressed, and headed for the Casa Marina. I got there a bit before Greg and Pete and ordered a cocktail from the patio bar while I waited. They arrived about the same time looking pensive and tired. I felt the same way. There was a strange sense of resignation, as though we all knew we were walking into something but had decided to go through with it anyway. So far, everything about the trip had gone smoothly other than a few hiccups, like the run-in with Customs in Jamaica, and being photographed by the DEA airplane. But we were almost home, and this was the last step for us. We just wanted to get it over with as quickly as possible.

We sat on deck until dark, knowing that somewhere nearby Johnny and his guys were watching us. What we didn't know was that the DEA was also watching us now, waiting for us to make a move. About an hour after sunset, we pulled anchor, headed out to sea, and turned on our running lights. Once we knew Johnny's guys were approaching us, we'd turn them off until we were unloaded and on our way to a berth in Oceanside Marina. Sounded simple enough, right?

Everything seemed fine during the first half hour after leaving our anchorage at the Casa Marina. Rather than mess around with raising and lowering sails, we just motored our way out to sea. There were some mild swells, but no big waves, and the boat moved quickly with a minimum of rolling and pitching. Greg and Pete put rubber fenders on both sides of the sailboat, so that both speedboats could tie up at the same time, and we could unload twice as quickly.

Once we knew we were in our unloading zone, we switched off our running lights. Within a minute, we heard the boats approaching, and in another minute, all hell broke loose.

Seemingly out of nowhere, two helicopters approached from both sides. We couldn't see them, but we could hear them coming up on us very quickly. They were running without lights, and against the night sky, they were as good as invisible. At the same time, the two speedboats were tying up on both sides of us. Johnny was in one of the boats.

"Start getting that shit out of there!" he screamed. "Move it!"

I was in a state of near panic. Both choppers were hovering above us, but I could barely see either one. They were very close, and the noise they made was deafening. I shouted to Greg and Pete below, and two of Johnny's men jumped aboard to help unload. With the choppers overhead, we started tossing bales onto the two speedboats as quickly as we could.

"What about them?" I screamed at Johnny, pointing overhead.

"Fuck 'em! They're after the load, and they can't do anything from the choppers except watch and let others know where we are. Just get it unloaded. They'll follow us."

"What'll happen to us?"

"You'll be empty. You aren't the main target. The load is the main target."

Suddenly, both helicopters turned on spotlights, flooding the deck and lighting up our entire unloading operation.

Johnny laughed. "Well, at least we can see what we're doing now," he shouted. "That's just a signal for other boats on the way here. They'll be more of a problem. Let's move it!"

It was mayhem. We were unloading our entire shipment right under the nose of two law enforcement helicopters as they hovered over us, bathing us in their spotlights. They were so close we could barely think straight through the steady thumping of the blades, and the adrenaline was pounding through my veins. My entire body was in overdrive, and for a split second I found myself marveling at what a great time I was having. It instantly struck me as very strange to be enjoying something like this, but that's exactly what happened. It was the biggest rush of my life, and I was totally enjoying it. I even remember laughing out loud, almost an adrenaline-fueled shout. Fuck dem boys. We're pirates.

Within another instant, I went back into work mode and focused my energy on getting as many bales to the skiff as quickly as I could. After an eternity, with the ear-crushing sound of the helicopter blades thumping directly overhead, and the harshness of the two spotlights turning everything bright white, we tossed the last bales onto the skiffs and quickly untied them. I saw three or four bales tumble off one of the boats and into the water. Nobody bothered to retrieve them, and they bobbed on the surface, disappearing into the dark. Both speedboats pulled away from the sailboat and sped away. As Johnny had predicted, the two helicopters immediately turned and started to follow the speedboats.

And just like that, as quickly as the mayhem had started, it ended. Suddenly we were completely alone again, the boat was empty, and it was quiet. We weren't anchored, and the boat was drifting free, but we were a mile from shore, and I knew there were no shoals or coral loggerheads in the area, so we took a few minutes to relax. I turned on a light below and looked at Greg and Pete. I had to laugh. When the lights came on, all I could see were two guys whose eyes were wide as saucers, completely flushed with adrenaline and still wired from their wildest experience to date. We all laughed nervously.

"Well, that was somewhat stimulating," I said. "Would anyone like a beer?"

TEN

TRIAL AND ERROR

We were still drifting free, with no running lights, but I didn't hear any boats in the area, nor did I see any other running lights. It seemed clear that law enforcement was focusing its efforts on getting the load, and not us. After sipping on our beers for a few minutes, we all calmed down a bit.

"What do you think, guys? Take her into the marina now? We could also just sail up the coast to another marina and put in tomorrow. That would give us time to clean up the boat, and we'd be home free."

"I just want to get off this thing," said Pete. "I want it to end tonight. I'm fried."

I looked at Greg. "What do you think?"

"I agree with Pete. Let's get to the marina. I think we're clear. Let's just get off this thing and clean it up in the morning."

I had my misgivings, and as the captain, I could override them both, but I was weary as well. I just wanted it to be over, and I wanted to sleep in my own bed. I should have trusted my instincts and continued up the coast to another marina, but I didn't.

We turned our running lights back on, and I set a course for the light at the head of the channel heading into Oceanside Marina. I should have had the guys clean up the boat a bit before we pulled in, as there was loose marijuana laying everywhere, easily a pound or two, that had spilled from the loosely packed bales as we'd unloaded them. It would have been easy to sweep it all up and spray all the surfaces with Lysol before entering the marina, but I was simply too tired to care at that point. All we could think about was being done with this trip, and we had tunnel vision.

My first warning sign that something wasn't right was the number of vehicles around the dock master's office at 9:00 in the evening. It was typically deserted. The second warning was seeing the light on inside the dock master's office. Gabe never stayed that late for any reason, and I could see several people moving around inside as we came down the channel. As I swung the boat around to dock, Gabe himself came out of the shack, which I found very odd. He smiled at me, and nodded, and I realized at that point that something was about to happen. Greg and Pete stepped ashore, tied up the boat, and then came back onboard.

"How are you tonight, Kelly?" asked Gabe.

I didn't answer immediately as I scanned the marina parking lot. I knew there were a bunch of men inside the dock master's office, but nobody else was on the dock.

"I'm good, Gabe. How about you?"

"Good. Feel free to stay here until morning. We can get you a slip then."

He was acting very formal and reserved, which I found unsettling. Something just wasn't right, but he wasn't telling me anything. He walked back to his office and went inside. I sat in the cockpit for a bit, looking around the marina. It was as quiet as it normally would be at this hour, but I was concerned about the cars and the people inside the dock master's shack. I watched for a while, and once or twice someone inside would walk to the window and look at me but then turn away. After a few minutes, I decided that I was being paranoid. From time to time, people would take beer to the dock master's shack after hours and drink with Gabe, and I finally convinced myself that he was just inside having beers with friends. After about ten minutes on deck, I went below. Greg and Pete were having another beer. I finally allowed myself to relax and pulled out a box of nice Jamaican cigars I'd purchased on the trip and passed them around.

"Gentlemen, to a successful trip, at least for us. Let's hope Johnny's boys get the load to safety, but for us, it's over. Time to celebrate."

I'd no sooner lit my cigar when I heard movement on the docks, and then the sound of several people all boarding the boat at once. The sailboat tipped toward the dock with the sudden addition of several bodies, and in an instant, people dressed in black shirts dropped into the hatches fore and aft, fully armed, and pointing guns at our heads. There were three of us, and at least six or eight of them, and every one of them was armed. It's a horrible feeling having several guns pressed to your head and knowing that any one of those guys might be a bit too excited and accidentally blow your brains out. Strangely, they all looked afraid of us, almost nervous, and overly aggressive with their commands, especially since we offered no resistance, and immediately raised our hands.

"Hey, guys. Easy now. Please calm down. We're not dangerous. We're not armed."

After a few long, tense moments, some calm returned. Nobody had spoken other than me.

The men kept their guns on us but backed up a bit to give us some space. I heard someone else board the boat, then a voice.

"Come up. One at a time."

I was closest to the main hatch, so I went first. Another man was in the cockpit, pointing a shotgun at me as I exited the hatch. Standing beside him was a shorter man with a black ball cap. He nodded toward the shore.

"Get off the boat, then kneel with your hands behind your head."

I stepped off the boat, kneeled, put my hands behind my back when instructed to, and then was handcuffed. This procedure was repeated with Greg and Pete until all three of us were on the dock, on our knees, handcuffed.

The shorter man with the black ball cap seemed to be the guy in charge. He stood before us and introduced himself.

"I'm Agent Seale. You're under arrest for conspiracy to smuggle and distribute illegal drugs. Do you understand these charges?"

We all said yes, and another agent read us our Miranda rights. "Stand up," said Agent Seale.

We tried to stand, but it was difficult with our hands behind our backs. Two other agents pulled us to our feet. Seale nodded toward a car.

"Put them in the back," he said.

The other agents led us to a large sedan, held the door while Greg, Pete, and I did our best to get into the car with our hands behind our backs, and then slammed the door on us. Seale climbed into the front seat, which was a single, large bench front seat.

"Are you comfortable?" he asked.

"Not exactly," I replied.

"Well, tough shit." He hit the button on the seat and slammed it back onto us with all the force he could muster. I remember thinking to myself that this guy was a real asshole, but I kept that opinion to myself, as I didn't want to make things worse.

We were driven to another location in the area, near one of the many Naval Station facilities in the area and taken to a large office. After sitting together for a bit in a lobby, we were all separated and taken to different rooms. We all knew we were about to be interrogated, and we'd planned for this moment, while hoping it would never happen.

Seale seemed to know that I was the captain, so he started with me. "Where's the shipment going?"

I shrugged. "I don't know what you're talking about."

The questioning continued, but I just kept shrugging and acting like I knew nothing. "What's all that loose weed doing on your boat?" he asked. I knew he was just fishing at that point.

"I don't know. Someone must have spilled their bag or something."

He was frustrated. I suspected Greg and Pete were getting a similar grilling in other rooms, and I knew they were playing dumb just like me. He asked a lot of specific questions about who I worked for, how much we'd been carrying, where we'd been, etc., but I just kept shaking my head and telling him that I didn't know what he was talking about. He finally gave up in frustration and left the room. Based on his angry behavior, I suspected that Johnny and his guys had managed to get away with the shipment, and that Seale had ended up empty-handed. I found myself smiling a little despite my situation. Had he managed to get the entire shipment, I doubted he would have wasted so much time grilling us to no avail. We would have been afterthoughts and kicked down the line for booking. The fact that the head of the operation had focused so much time on our arrest and questioning suggested that the shipment had not been confiscated, and Johnny and his crew were still at large. I knew we were about to get locked up, so it would be several days before I'd know anything for sure, but at that point, I was confident that the shipment was safe, at least for the time being.

After being held in the DEA facility until morning, we were transported down to the county jail at daybreak, where we learned we'd be in a large, general population holding cell with all sorts of criminals. None of us liked that idea at all and decided we'd all have to have each other's backs. It was a huge cell, about 1,000 square feet, filled with bunks. There was a large communal shower and toilet area, and we'd be in there for an undetermined length of time until someone could raise bail and secure our release. We hadn't yet heard the specific charges against us, but knew they couldn't be too bad, as we hadn't been caught with any large amounts of weed. When we were released into the large holding cell, we found a few unoccupied bunks all in a group and took them over.

We looked around. All eyes were on us, the three new guys being brought in by the Feds. I remember scanning the room looking for anyone who might be trouble. I also had enough smarts by then to look around for anyone I felt might be a DEA informant or plant, who'd been put there to see if they could get any more information out of us. I warned Greg and Pete not to talk to anyone about our trip. If engaged in a conversation, we would just keep it light and vague. Our story was that we'd been busted with a small amount of weed, and that was it.

The first day in the holding cell came and went without incident. We didn't receive any calls from anyone, which surprised me. I assumed Garry or someone would at least touch base with us to give us a heads-up on what was happening. Pete's girlfriend Barb was probably worried sick when Pete didn't show up at their house. Same for Greg, whose girlfriend hadn't joined us on the trip. I lived alone, so there wouldn't be anyone waiting on me. The other occupants of the holding cell seemed harmless, although we kept our eyes on a few, and we made certain that one of us was always awake while the other two slept. When we took a shower, we did it one at a time, with the other two standing guard. We didn't want any trouble, and we didn't want any surprises. More than that, we didn't want to find ourselves embroiled in some altercation that would keep us in the holding cell any longer than necessary.

The second day came and went, and still no contact from outside. We talked amongst ourselves and began to wonder what was going on. Pete made a phone call to Barb to let her know what was going on, and to ask if she'd heard anything from Garry. She hadn't but said she'd try to contact him. We didn't use his real name on the phone, as we suspected the jailhouse phone line was bugged.

On the morning of the third day, we were summoned to get ready for our arraignment, where we'd hear the charges against us. We only had the clothes we'd been wearing when we were arrested: shorts, t-shirts, and flip-flops. As we hadn't officially become prisoners of the county jail system, we had not been given the standard prison garb, so we'd been living in the same clothes for three days. We thought about asking for some clean prison jumpsuits for our arraignment, but we decided to just go as we were. Showing up in an orange jumpsuit made us look guilty, we thought. We just wanted to look like sailors.

Around ten o'clock on the third day, we were transported by a small van down to the county courthouse and escorted into the courtroom. We were the only people there, other than court staff and a cocky-looking rooster of a man waiting at the defense table. He introduced himself as Don, our lawyer. He immediately huddled with us and informed us that he'd been hired by Garry, and that everything would be taken care of regarding our arrest and upcoming trial.

The arraignment was quick. We were charged with two felonies: intent to smuggle and intent to distribute. The judge asked if we had any questions, which we didn't, and then we were allowed to talk privately with Don in a small side room, where he told us that our bail was being met, and that we'd probably be released the next day. This was the first we'd heard anything. Although I was a bit frustrated that we'd sat in jail for several days without hearing from anyone, I also understood why Garry didn't try to contact us. He was simply keeping himself out of the equation and not drawing attention to himself or to Luis's operation.

A half hour later, we were back in jail, but at least we knew what was happening and when we'd be released. In the few days we'd been in the holding cell, only a few of the other prisoners made any attempt to speak with us. Most kept their distance and treated us with a certain amount of respect. They'd watched us arrive, escorted by five men wearing blue windbreakers with DEA on the back, and it made an impression. One of the prisoners who spoke to us said the other guys were a bit intimidated by us, and we had stature in the group. We found this amusing. We were worried about having to defend ourselves from other prisoners and instead learned we were given top-dog status without even knowing it.

On the fourth day, we were summoned by a guard and escorted out to a lobby, where we learned our bail had been met, and we were being released. Once again, it was Don meeting us, and not Garry, which we understood by now. Don took us to lunch and chatted amicably about the case, joking and laughing about how he loved to represent smugglers. I didn't know much about lawyering, but I was surprised at his cavalier attitude, which didn't strike me as very professional. I could see he was trying to be cool with us, but I had no intention of telling him anything other than to directly answer any questions pertinent to our case. After lunch, Don paid the tab, shook our hands, and told us he'd be in touch about our trial date.

"Are we actually going to go to court to fight two felony charges?" I asked.

"I'm working on a plea bargain. They came up empty-handed, other than the loose chaff laying around the boat. They didn't get anything."

This was the first we'd heard that the shipment was safe. Johnny and his guys had somehow evaded the helicopters. We'd learn all the details later, but at that point, we were relieved to learn that the shipment hadn't been confiscated.

I looked at Greg and Pete. They had slight grins on their faces. Without the shipment, the DEA really didn't have much of a case against us. It would be difficult to make felony charges stick when all they had was a pound of loose weed they'd swept off the floor of the boat.

"So, that's it for now," said Don. "I'll be in touch about your court date, which will be in county court in Miami."

"Why a county court?" I asked. "We were arrested by Feds."

"That's another good sign. If this was a big case where they wanted publicity, you'd be looking at a federal court. The fact that they kicked this down to a county court tells me they don't have much faith in this case going anywhere. The charges have been re-filed by the state, so they're not Federal DEA charges. They flubbed it and got nothing. They want this one to get swept under the rug and be gone. It's egg on their face."

One week later, Don contacted us to let us know that he'd reached a plea bargain agreement. All we'd have to do in court is plead guilty to misdemeanor possession of an ounce of marijuana and put ourselves at the mercy of the court. He was certain we'd get off lightly.

We learned that our court date would be taking place less than a month after our arrest. One of the goals of Bush's Task Force was a steady stream of charges and court cases, and the courts were busy. The three of us quickly went back to our normal lives for a few weeks, and during this time we never heard from Garry or anyone associated with our group. It was as if they had ceased to exist. Greg, Pete, and I talked about it and realized that this was Garry's way of isolating himself from any exposure. If anyone was watching us, and we were certain this was taking place, then he didn't want to be seen with us. The shipment had survived, and we were certain that the DEA was watching us to see if we contacted anyone. Agent Seale didn't strike me as the type of guy who just quit on things. An entire shipment of weed had managed to get away from him on his watch, and we were certain he was still trying to track it down.

Our court date arrived, and the three of us drove up to Miami. We didn't know what to expect. We were nervous but confident in a quick resolution based upon the information we'd received from Don. Pete, Greg, and I were shocked by the size of the courtroom. It looked more like an auditorium (it was, we learned later), and it was filled almost entirely with men. Looking around, we saw a few women, but they looked like lawyers or legal staff. The overwhelming majority of the people in the room were defendants, just like us. It quickly became clear that this courtroom was set up to push cases through, as quickly as they could be called.

Don checked in with a woman seated at a table near the front of the makeshift courtroom and came back to us. We were the eleventh case on the docket.

"What does that mean for a timeframe?" I asked Don.

He looked at me and shrugged. "I have no idea, but I get the impression things will move quickly."

Within minutes after taking our seats, the judge arrived. We all stood and then were seated. The judge, the Honorable Peter Palermo, was introduced, and we took our seats as he quickly got the proceedings into high gear. The first case was a freighter crew from a Colombian vessel, caught with 60,000 pounds of marijuana. The judge heard a statement from both the prosecution and the defense, had both attorneys approach his bench, and quickly passed sentence. The case was settled in minutes. We were stunned. This judge was in a hurry and wasn't messing around. The next few cases were similar. Groups of men on boats caught with large amounts of marijuana or cocaine. Foreign nationals were handed over for deportation and extradition, and Americans were given jail sentences, typically around four or five years in the Florida State penitentiary if arrested and charged by the Florida Marine Patrol or Coast Guard. Our case moved closer, and less than an hour had passed.

Within ninety minutes of the beginning of the court being called to order, our case came to trial. We weren't prepared for what was about to happen.

Judge Palermo asked the clerk to read the charges.

The clerk started reading. He got our names right, and that was about it. As for our charges, we heard him say, "The defendants were arrested in the Miami International Airport with seven kilos of cocaine in their possession."

We all looked at Don, who looked very confused and flustered.

"Your Honor, those are not the correct charges." He glanced over at the assistant district attorney on the prosecution's side, then back at the judge. "I'd specifically negotiated a plea bargain agreement a few weeks ago, for misdemeanor possession of marijuana, with the alleged crime taking place in Key West, not the Miami International Airport."

Judge Palermo looked confused and annoyed. We looked at Don. I didn't know much about the law, but this seemed like a great time to ask for a mistrial. Maybe I'd watched too many television shows, but someone had screwed up, and it seemed like a great time to wrap things up. But Don pressed ahead, which surprised me. He corrected the clerk.

"My clients were arrested in Key West on suspicion of importing and distributing marijuana. Their case has nothing to do with cocaine or the Miami International Airport."

He looked over at the district attorney, who looked even more confused, especially since Palermo was now glaring at him.

"Uhm . . . I'm not sure what happened here. I had specifically met with the Defense, and we had in fact agreed upon a plea bargain deal, for misdemeanor possession of one ounce. The alleged crime took place in Key West, your Honor. I have no idea how the paperwork got so screwed up."

Judge Palermo was pissed and wasn't hiding it. He'd been on a roll until our case came up. He looked at the DA.

"So, tell me the original charges, and the details of the plea bargain. Make it quick," he asked.

The DA quickly mentioned the two original felonies, noting a lack of evidence to support them, and then the plea bargain deal he'd reached with Don. I was still waiting for Don to ask for a mistrial, but he seemed more focused on getting the facts straight, which baffled me.

Judge Palermo had heard enough. He looked at Don and asked how we'd plead to the plea bargain agreement.

"They plead guilty, your Honor."

Palermo looked at us closely for the first time. He'd just spent the past hour sentencing hardened criminals to five years in jail for smuggling, and they'd been caught with thousands of pounds of marijuana and cocaine in their possession. He looked at us over his half-moon reading glasses, looking confused. We were all dressed like we'd just left a Ralph Lauren store. I was dressed in new khakis and a blue seersucker shirt with button-down collar. Greg was in a navy polo shirt, with khakis. Pete was also wearing new khakis with a light-blue chambray shirt. We'd all been to a barber recently and were nicely trimmed and clean-shaven. We might have even looked a bit pensive and frightened, partially by design. Palermo looked at us longer than he'd looked at any defendants so far that morning, and then shook his head, almost laughing, but not quite. He slammed down his gavel.

"One year's probation. Case closed." He nodded at the clerk's desk. "Get your paperwork and get down the hall to see the probation officer."

In the probation office, the probation officer looked at our paperwork and made a face.

He made it obvious that he didn't want to be bothered with having to travel to Key West to check on us. He pulled a coin from his pocket.

"Heads is non-reporting probation. Tails is reporting." He flipped the coin but didn't show it to us. "Heads it is."

He smiled and had us quickly sign some paperwork. He told us that if we kept our noses clean for the entire year, our records would be expunged in five years, and there'd be no records of the arrest or the probation, at least not records available to anyone outside law enforcement. He shook our hands and told us to have a nice life and stay out of trouble. The entire process had taken about ten minutes.

And just like that, we were free.

At this point, a smart man would have counted his lucky stars and walked away. I'd had a blast, made a nice chunk of change, bought a great little seaworthy sailboat and a cool BMW motorcycle, and had a crazy story to tell. It should have been time to get back to a normal life, get a job, and get serious about a career. That's what a smart man would have done.

But I was not a smart man.

ELEVEN

COCAINE COWBOY

In the aftermath of the trial, I found myself despondent. After two years of living a high-octane lifestyle, I suddenly found myself with nothing to do. I had a safe deposit box filled with money, so I wouldn't have to find work anytime soon, and I had plenty of time, so I could sail and drink and ride up the Keys on my motorcycle any time I wanted, but I grew listless and bored. I knew I was done being a smuggling captain, but I wasn't done with the lifestyle.

There was also the matter of getting paid for the trip. I knew the load had made it safely out of the Keys, although it had been hidden on a small mangrove island for several weeks until things quieted down with the DEA and the Task Force operations. I spoke with Johnny, and learned that they'd been chased by the helicopters, but outran them in the dark. The helicopters had apparently alerted two other speedboats filled with Marine Patrol and DEA agents, and somehow the chase helicopters had confused the DEA boats with Johnny's speedboats, and the confusion allowed them to get away with the load.

They'd run into Boca Chica channel, passed under the Boca Chica Channel bridge, and into the backcountry, where they had vanished. Johnny and his friends had grown up in the Keys and had owned boats since they were in high school. They knew the backcountry blindfolded, and this wasn't their first rodeo running weed from the authorities. They had a small mangrove island they used for storing weed. The island had no real solid ground that was above water all the time, and they'd built a small platform at the center of it where they stored the weed, which was covered with waterproof tarps, and then covered again with military-style camouflage tarps that looked just like more mangrove trees from the air. They'd taken the shipment there, left it for a few weeks while making sure to keep an eye on it daily. When things quieted down, they'd met up with Garry's hired couple and got it to shore. It had been loaded into a camper, which had been driven up the Keys, up through central Florida, and then up the coast to the northeast, where it was delivered to the distributors.

I was angry that we hadn't been paid and that Garry had made no mention of being paid.

I confronted him on the matter. He responded with anger, which caught me off guard. "Getting greedy now, are we?" he said. "We just spent over $30,000 on bail and court costs for you guys. That money had to come from somewhere. Where do you think that money came from?"

"You always made it sound like we were covered, no matter what. You never told me that we would basically be surrendering our pay if caught."

"That's the way it works. We have a business to run, and you became a big expense."

"But the load wasn't confiscated. I was under the impression that if we lost the load, we didn't get paid. We didn't lose the load."

"A new set of circumstances arose," he replied. "No, the load wasn't confiscated, but you guys were arrested, and we had to hire lawyers. They don't come cheap."

He looked angry and aggressive, like he wanted me to challenge him further. I backed off but wasn't happy. I made plans to talk to him again, this time in Miami, and I was hoping that Luis would be there to hear me out. For some dumb reason, I felt Luis would side with me.

I arrived in Miami for the meeting, but Luis wasn't there. Garry was sitting on the couch, and a man I recognized as one of Luis's hit men was sitting on the couch beside him, staring at me from the moment I entered the room. Before I even sat down, I'd conceded that I wasn't going to be getting paid for this trip. The only reason Garry would have Luis's man there was to intimidate me with the threat of violence, and it worked. Garry brought me a cold cocktail from the kitchen, and he was all smiles.

He knew the matter was settled, and I quickly finished my drink and left the condo after some small talk without ever mentioning money. I wasn't going to get myself beat up or killed over money. I returned to Key West, even more despondent.

In the weeks that followed, I drank constantly and used a lot of drugs. It was during this time that Garry, in an apparent show of no-hard-feelings, contacted me and told me to stop by next time I was in Coconut Grove, as he wanted to talk to me about something. He acted as though everything was just fine, and it pissed me off. But I was curious and decided to go meet with him anyway. Although I had a motorcycle now and loved to ride it almost everywhere, I still didn't like riding it in Miami traffic, so whenever I went to Garry's, I would just walk into the airport in Key West, buy a cheap ticket to Miami on the next Air Florida flight out of town, and Garry or Sarah would pick me up at the airport. Flights were cheap and there were many daily flights between Miami and Key West, so I found it much easier and quicker to fly.

Sarah picked me up at the airport. It was the first time I'd seen her since she got off the boat in Jamaica to fly home, and I was happy to see her. She seemed genuinely interested to see me as well, and we had a great chat on the way back to the condo.

Garry stood up from the couch when I entered. He was all smiles, but he was usually all smiles, even when he wasn't in a good mood.

"How are you, buddy?" He grinned and slapped me on the shoulder. "Have a seat. Let me get you a drink." He looked at Sarah and nodded to the kitchen. She walked to the kitchen and mixed me a drink.

"So. How the hell have you been? Are you holding up?"

"I'm fine. Just need to find something to do. Still trying to settle back into civilian life, and it's weird."

He laughed way too hard. "I know how that goes," he said. "I've been trying for the past decade."

"So, what's this thing you want to talk about?" I asked.

He waved at me to sit down while he took a sip of his drink. I saw a gram of coke on the glass coffee tabletop, with a few lines cut out. Garry saw me looking and motioned to them.

"Help yourself! Relax first. We have plenty of time. You can even spend the night if you want."

I hadn't planned on that, but I still liked being around Sarah, so I decided I'd stay. I did two lines of coke and sat back into the deep couch as I felt the rush hitting my brain. Garry always had pure coke, right from the kilo, uncut. Once you've done pure coke, you can spot the stuff that's cut with speed and other junk immediately.

We spent the next hour just making small talk and discussing the past trip. We really hadn't had a chance to talk about it, and he wanted to hear everything that had happened the night of our arrest, right down to the smallest details. He seemed particularly interested in the DEA agent who'd led the arrest and did the interrogation.

"So, what was that guy's name again?"

"Seale. Not a nice guy."

Garry smiled. "I think he has a brother or relative who's a big honcho in Washington."

"You know of him?" I asked.

"Yeah," said Garry. "He's a cowboy, though. Got his position through a family contact, but he's too much of a cowboy to be in his position. He got greedy with you guys. They were on to you before you even left the Casa Marina anchorage. He could have had you, your crew, and a loaded boat, but he apparently has a vendetta with Johnny's crew and wanted to catch them with everything, which is why they focused on following the loaded speedboats, and not just busting you when you went back to the boat."

"How do you know all this?" I asked.

"Luis has a contact. Some kid he put through college, who is in the DEA and now works on the Task Force. The kid speaks fluent Spanish and is part Cuban, so he knew he'd be assigned to work south Florida at some point." Garry laughed and rocked his head a bit.

That didn't surprise me. Anyone with Luis's money and business acumen would do the same, and it made perfect sense. The more I learned about Luis, the more I became aware that he was a man who played the long game and played it *way* better than most could even imagine.

You might think you were two steps ahead of him, but in fact, he was five steps ahead of you, allowing you to *think* you were ahead of him. He may have been a criminal, but I marveled at his ability to be completely invisible to law enforcement while always knowing their next step. I'd worked for him for two years, and only knew him by one name, which I knew wasn't even his real name. He was a true ghost, and one talented businessman. I can only imagine how he would have fared in the private sector.

I was hoping Garry would have a change of heart and pay me something for the trip. I kept asking about the load, and if everything went smoothly, hoping he was getting the hint, and knowing I wasn't going to press him further on the matter.

"That's a done deal. It's a wrap. Nothing farther to discuss on that matter," he said.

I shrugged. I looked over at Sarah, who was sitting on the couch beside Garry. She was smiling at me, a genuine smile that made me feel good despite all the frustration of dealing with Garry and money.

"Let's order some food!" he said suddenly.

"Before we do, can you tell me what you had in mind? You said you wanted to talk to me about something."

"Let's order, then we'll talk while we're waiting."

After calling in our food order, Garry sat back on the couch and sighed deeply, then smiled.

"How'd you like to make some money?"

I was caught off guard. I was expecting him to give me some cash, anything, for taking the risks on the last trip, but that wasn't going to happen. If I wanted more money, I was going to have to go back to work for it.

"What did you have in mind?"

"You have lots of friends in Key West, right? Everyone likes coke. How'd you like to move coke for me? You already have a clientele. Just stop giving it to them for free, as I know you do, and start selling it to them." He clapped his hands and laughed. "Don't be so nice. Sell it to them. Stop trying to be the good guy."

He wasn't wrong. Virtually every single person I knew in Key West did coke. Most were opportunistic and didn't buy much themselves but instead hung around with people who did.

Since I started smuggling, I always had some of Garry's coke on hand, as he sold me uncut grams cheaply, and often just gave it to me. I'd often cut it with Vitamin B12 and make one gram into three. It still worked great, and it was better than cutting with cheap speed. It also made the coke last longer, and the cut stuff was what I was often sharing with my partying friends, while keeping the pure, uncut stuff for myself, or to share with close friends.

I was intrigued, to put it lightly. Here was a chance to have unlimited access to all the coke I could ever want, while providing the means to continue my outlaw lifestyle without risking arrest and a jail sentence if I got caught on a boat with tons of weed. I had given up being a smuggling boat captain as I didn't want to risk another arrest for the same offense.

Suddenly, I found myself thinking about becoming a coke dealer, and the thought of arrest and prison didn't even cross my mind. As I said earlier, a smart man would have walked away, but I wasn't a smart man. To this day, I'm still not sure where my critical thinking skills had gone, but they were completely absent at that time. I was about to get back in the game, and I was excited about it. I was incapable of thinking more than thirty minutes into the future.

After a great Thai takeout dinner, the three of us sat around the coffee table doing more coke and laughing about the trip. I'd already forgiven him for not paying me and was excited about the prospect of selling coke. Within an hour after making the decision to sell, I'd already figured out what my operation would look like, and I ran it by Garry and Sarah.

"Okay. I already have several friends who can move large amounts, and don't mind the exposure. I will limit my exposure for the most part by dealing primarily with them."

"How much do you think you can move at one time?" asked Garry.

"Probably up to ten ounces a month as a best-case scenario, but real-istically a bit less," I replied. I would be dealing with uncut coke. He was going to front it to me at $1,800 per ounce. I was going to ask for three ounces at a time, which would mean I'd immediately be on the hook for $5,400 cash, payable directly to Garry every month. I'm sure he had some markup on there, so he was making hundreds per ounce just by handing it to me. I planned to take those three ounces, keep about a half an ounce of pure, uncut coke for my personal use, and then add B12 to the remainder, making it into about six or seven ounces, where it would still be effective and work just fine. I had been told that B12 was a "safe" cutting agent, and it could be purchased at health food stores, so I was convinced there was no danger.

Once cut, I could then mark up the ounces to $2,000 per ounce, or whatever the market would take, and make a very nice profit for myself every month. Some quick figuring on a calculator told me I could gross over $10,000 a month easily, possibly more, with $5,400 going back to Garry, and I would keep the rest. I could sell three cut ounces for a markup, and pay Garry from that, and the rest would be solid profit. By selling it wholesale in full ounces to a few close friends, I'd be insulating myself from the street-level sales and operating from a safe position. I discussed this with Garry, and he seemed impressed.

"I've taught you well!" he said with a laugh.

I wasn't sure it was anything I'd learned from him, however. Two years of being a smuggler had taught me to think things through and always cover your ass. If being safe and insulated from scrutiny took a bit of your profit away, then by all means go that route. Garry always said it was the greedy people who got caught, and I had to agree with him.

We talked, laughed, drank, and snorted at least a full gram of coke well into the night. By the end of the evening, I was genuinely having fun again, and enjoying his company, made more enjoyable by the presence of Sarah, who smiled at me a lot. I knew she was loyal to Garry, but I welcomed any attention she sent my way. I had no intention of crossing any lines at that point, but I really enjoyed flirting with her.

The following morning over breakfast, Garry handed me three tightly wrapped ounces of coke. They were wrapped so tightly that they felt almost firm. I was going to hide them on my body somewhere and fly back to the Keys with them. I stood in the bathroom with the three bags, trying to find a safe, comfortable place to carry them, but everything seemed too obvious or risky. I tried duct-taping them to my body in several locations, but nothing seemed comfortable or seemed like it would hold if I started sweating.

"Why not just stuff them in your underwear?" asked Garry.

I'd never thought of that. It hadn't seemed like a very sanitary place to put something that people would be snorting up their noses, even though it would be in sealed bags. After some thought, though, I decided it would be a great idea. There was just one problem. I hadn't worn underwear or socks since moving to the Keys. I found them too hot, uncomfortable and restricting. Shortly after moving there, I'd gone full 'commando,' and ditched the undergarments in favor of comfort and breathability. After a quick run to a local mall, I returned with two 3-packs of white briefs, wrapped the three ounces up tightly in cellophane wrap, and tucked the package down the front of my underwear. It looked comical. I looked like a rock star, and after sharing a good laugh with Garry and Sarah, I readjusted the package a bit, moved it down farther, and decided I could get through a basic pat-down easily, as that would be the one place where I wouldn't be patted down.

Sarah and Garry dropped me off at the Miami International Airport later that day to catch a return flight to Key West. I was coked up, smoked up, and feeling cocky again. There was something exhilarating about walking through the airport past hundreds of people with three ounces of pure cocaine packed beside my private parts. It felt surreal, and it was exciting as hell. I was back in the game once again, and this time around, I'd be transporting cocaine between Miami and Key West, courtesy of Air Sunshine.

For the next several months, things went smoothly. After picking up my three or four ounces in Miami and returning to the Keys, I'd take several ounces, cut them, and then sell them wholesale to friends who were willing to break them down into grams for resale, which is where they made their profit. The three people buying the bulk of the coke were friends I trusted, and they understood how the chain of possession worked. If they got caught, they took the fall. You never gave up the guy above you in the distribution chain. That was the theory, but in reality, people often turned and gave up their suppliers. But I trusted my friends to be smart and do the right thing, and I'm almost certain they would have done the right thing, should it have ever come to that point.

I was getting my coke fronted to me by Garry, who knew I wasn't going to screw him over. I was just one step removed from Luis, and I didn't want that sort of heat coming after me for anything. As soon as I sold my ounces wholesale and had Garry's money, I immediately put it aside until I could get it to him. Once put aside, I never touched it again until I handed him the envelope. He once told me I was the kind of guy he liked to have working for him, as I was reliable and consistent.

"Most of the people in this business at your level are heavy users, and that's why they're doing it—so they have their own supply. But using your own product is the quickest way to wreck your life. It's good to see you have that under control," he told me.

What he didn't realize is that I was using heavily and drinking as well, and it was about to start catching up to me.

This new life as a coke dealer was much to my liking. I missed the open water sailing trips, but I felt like I had more control over outcomes as a coke dealer. I had a simple distribution chain of friends whom I trusted, and I trusted Garry to always have the product I needed. Within months, my little operation was a consistent and highly-profitable money machine for everyone involved. Garry had a seller who never missed a payment, and I had sellers I trusted who always paid me upfront, upon delivery. I could have made a lot more money if I'd done more of the street-level sales myself, but I was determined to make a bit less money to remain safe. I admired how well Luis had insulated himself from any connection to his own business, and it was a lesson I'd taken to heart and applied to my own little business operation.

Life seemed great. My slip fee at the marina was about $125 a month, and I had no other regular expenses except gas for the motorcycle and food. I was clearing about $6,000 a month during this time (a very nice income in the early 1980s), and you might assume that I would have saved some of it. You would be wrong. I can't even remember what I spent it on, but I burned through so much cash every month that it still makes me sick. I was always going into bars and buying rounds for the entire place, taking vacations and flying almost everywhere, loaning money to people I knew would never pay me back, and buying anything and everything that caught my eye, whether I needed it or not. I didn't even bother to open a checking account or give myself a monthly stipend to control the flow. I had a safe-deposit box in an old bank at the corner of Front and Duval Streets, and I went there regularly to drop off and pick up cash as needed. I never bothered to count the money. There always seemed to be lots of money in the safe deposit box, and if I couldn't see the bottom of the tray, I felt like it would never run out.

Life likes to throw us some interesting curveballs, and always at unexpected times. On one trip through the Miami International Airport, on my way to the Air Sunshine departing gate, I stopped for a coffee. I had some time, so rather than walk with a hot coffee, I sat on a small bench in the middle of the concourse, which was surrounded by arrival and departure gates. When I was making the trips from Miami to Key West carrying cocaine, I never really thought about running into someone I knew in the concourse. I'd done it a few times, but it was an uncommon occurrence, and typically someone I knew as an acquaintance only, so I could just wave, say a quick hello, and be on my way. When flying back to the Keys on my coke runs, I was usually high and had done at least several lines of coke before getting to the airport and generally avoided talking to anyone unless necessary. As I sipped my coffee, I saw a woman stand up in one of the gate seating areas and walk toward the window. Even with her back to me, she looked familiar, and I was intrigued. After a few moments, she turned around, and of all the places in that large concourse where she could have looked, she looked right at me. It took me a few seconds to realize it was Tiana, the woman whom I'd met in Key West, the same woman who'd hitched a ride to Cozumel with us. It was the same beautiful Tiana I'd thought about often, wondering if I'd ever see her again, wondering what might have happened if we'd known each other for longer than a few days.

I think she was as caught off-guard as I was. She stared at me for several seconds, a look of confusion on her face, and then broke into a huge, beautiful smile. She immediately began walking toward me. Oddly, I felt my heart sink. Part of me was delighted to see her, but I also knew I had a flight to catch, and carrying cocaine made me very nervous and a bit jumpy. I had always hoped to cross paths with her again, but not under those circumstances. She reached me and threw her arms around my neck, hugged me, and kissed me on the cheek.

"How have you been? Still living the sailing life?"

"Yes." I tried my best to act normal. "Living at Oceanside Marina, currently. What are you up to? Where are you off to, I should probably ask?"

"Belize," she said with a smile and a sweep of her arm. "Meeting my family for a small gathering. They have a time-share."

I was nervous and jittery from the coke and just plain paranoid with three ounces of pure coke on my body. I know I was acting a bit odd. I told her how great it was to run into her, but I could see some concern beginning to cloud her eyes as we made small talk. She squeezed my hand, and it calmed me down.

"Are you okay?" she asked. She was genuinely concerned. "You seem a bit jumpy."

I laughed. "Yeah, well I am."

"Anything I should be worried about?"

I decided to be totally honest. I was curious how she'd react, and I wanted to see how she treated me when we weren't in an idyllic setting.

"I'd love to talk more, but I'm sort of . . . carrying right now. A lot. That's why I'm nervous."

A flash of alarm spread over her face, and she stepped back a bit but still held my hand.

"Are you okay right now?"

"Well, I'm a bit buzzed and nervous."

"I can see that," she said. "Are you going to be okay?"

The way she asked, I knew she was asking about my long-term well-being.

"I hope so. I surely hope so."

I could tell she didn't want to hang around me too long but didn't want to be rude and rush off. She was understandably nervous about being next to someone carrying cocaine. She took a pen and card from her purse, and wrote down a telephone number, then handed me the card.

"I hope you'll call me sometime." She paused and looked deeply into my eyes. "Whenever you're done doing what you're doing."

We held each other's gaze for a long moment. In that moment, I realized that I was assessing everything I knew about her, how I felt about her, and if I wanted to take another step. I looked at her and saw the type of woman I'd always dreamed about, someone with a deep sense of adventure, a love for life, a willingness to chase crazy dreams and enjoy every second. I realized she was a lot like me, but looking into her eyes, I also saw that she would eventually want a more stable life, a family, a reliable husband, and enough stability to live a good life without major struggles. I know she was assessing me the same way—I could see it in her eyes. I realized, even at that moment, that she wasn't seeing what she was looking for, at least not at that moment in time. I still didn't know what I wanted my future to hold, and I could tell that she was seeing that uncertainty as well. We were a lot alike and very attracted to each other, but we both stood there looking at each other and deciding whether it was a relationship with a future. She had given me her phone number, so there might have been a bit of hope on her part that I'd grow out of whatever I was doing and become a more responsible adult. I loved the way she was looking at me, and I really wanted to see her again. I vowed to myself, right at that moment, that I'd become a better man, because I would have to be that man to win her heart.

She looked over her shoulder toward her departure gate. "I'd better get going."

"Me, too." I looked at my watch. "I have a plane to catch shortly."

She grabbed my hands again and squeezed them.

"It was great to see you again." She smiled. "Even under your stressful circumstances."

"It was great to see you as well. I've thought a lot about you since Cozumel. I had accepted that it was just going to be one of those 'ships passing in the night' things," I said.

She laughed. "I thought the same. I thought it was best that way. But sometimes the Universe just throws you back at someone, just in case you want a second try."

We held each other's gaze for a long time. She was amazing, and my head was spinning. I didn't want to bid farewell, so she said it for both of us. She kissed me goodbye.

"Call me sometime. Call when you're done with all this, and when you're certain you're done with all this," she said.

"I will. I promise."

I walked to my departure gate, elated and filled with a sense of purpose, determined to change my life and become a responsible citizen. On the flight home, I pulled out the card several times and read it. Just her first name, and her phone number, on the back of a business card for a quick-print shop in Hialeah, a suburb of Miami.

I landed in Key West a few hours later, took a cab back to the marina, and changed clothes. I forgot about the card, threw my khaki dungarees in the wash, and didn't remember the card again until I found it in a wad when I emptied the dryer. The wad disintegrated when I tried to unfold it, as did my hopes for a better future with Tiana when my smuggling days were over. I thought about her often in those days and still find myself thinking about her every few years, wondering what became of her. I always imagine she married an investment banker from somewhere in New England, has two or three kids, a summer home outside New York City, and that she still likes to sail, and maybe thinks of me once in a while when she's on the water.

I returned to Key West and back to my life as a cocaine distributor. I liked to think of myself more as a middleman than a dealer. There was no real distinction between the two, but it made me feel a bit better about myself. I was now drinking every day, often stoned and drunk by noon on an average day. It didn't strike me as a bad thing, just a natural part of living in the Keys. Personal freedom was a big thing to islanders, and we wanted to live any way we pleased without interference. Even close friends would give you a lot of slack in these situations, sometimes too much. I had a few friends express concern about my increasing drug and alcohol abuse, but they never pushed too hard. I assured them I had it under control. I'd convinced myself that since I wasn't drinking to deal with bad things, I could just stop whenever I wanted. I knew I could stop cold turkey, but I also knew I wasn't ready to and still had a long way to go before I reached that point. That's one of the problems with substance abuse, I learned. You always think you're in control, right up until you discover that you're not.

I became a regular at several bars around town and had grown to know most of the staff well. One of my favorite bars was on Front Street, a very nice place named Billie's Bar. Two of the bartenders had become friends, and I went there often. Kim and Joann were both from Pennsylvania (Philly and Manheim, if I recall), and I always enjoyed talking to them. It became one of my favorite bars, and I soon found myself really liking Joann a lot. For reasons I didn't realize until later, I never asked her out, but had always wanted to. She was a sweetheart, a tall, fun-loving gal who was nicknamed "Tan Joann," as she always had a great tan. I went there often to see her, but I think the reason I never asked her out was because I knew I wasn't that reliable as a dating guy, and I didn't want to do anything to hurt her if she had said yes. I didn't even trust myself to always do the right thing in those days. I partied all the time and often went home with women I'd meet in bars, mostly tourist women who seemed to love hooking up with a local guy who lived on a boat. I think I knew that I couldn't be the guy Joann wanted, so I didn't try to be. I felt better just being a friend. Her opinion of me mattered, and I didn't want to do anything to damage it.

While hanging around in the local bars, I started to recognize some of the patrons. When I'd been arrested by the DEA and held for questioning, I had been in the same room with about fifteen different agents, and I remember studying them all carefully to remember their faces in case I ever saw them again. Now that I was out and about again and enjoying a broad social life in Key West's finest bars, I started seeing these DEA agents, mostly in pairs. They dressed like tourists but clearly weren't. I was surprised that none of them seemed to recognize me, but they hadn't seemed as intent on remembering me as I had on remembering them. Over time, I began to see them regularly in the bars and made a point of letting the bartenders know, and in turn, they'd quietly let certain local customers know as well. Over several months, I must have recognized at least twelve of the agents who'd been present when I was arrested, and I made certain that the staff of every bar they frequented was made aware of who they were.

After I decided to sell coke, I began to learn the downside of having lots of money and no idea what I wanted to do with my life. It was easy to drink, smoke weed, and snort coke every day because I had nothing to do. I'd been writing all this time, but until this point, I was primarily a journal writer. I simply sat down on a regular basis and wrote whatever came into my head. It was fun, relaxing and very therapeutic. As my drug and alcohol use increased, I found my journaling becoming erratic and nonsensical, so I stopped. Without the journaling, I gave up the one bit of continuity that held my life together and began the start of my free-fall.

I still wrote but began trying to write short stories. I'd written some in high school and college, but they were strained attempts at an accepted form, and not very good. The stories I began to write during my sub-stance abuse were worse, far worse. I'd find myself enamored with an idea that might have popped into my head at 2 A.M., and then I'd spend a week maniacally trying to turn it into a coherent story, as seen through the eyes and mind of someone who was perpetually hungover, stoned and high, which was not a great combination for success. I still have most of those stories, some scribbled on legal pads, some carefully typed on an old manual typewriter, and others still in scribbled note form, ideas that never fully bloomed. Looking back at these attempts years later, I managed to get one good story from the entire period, and the rest will remain what they became: artifacts from a particularly bad period of my life.

Because I didn't have a job and because I lived in a marina, I often had the opportunity for temporary jobs on boats. The word around the marina was that I was a competent boat captain, although unlicensed, and was willing to work as skipper or crew wherever needed. My position as an unemployed pirate came in handy during this time. I found work with a small sailboat charter company hiring myself out as a 'advisory skipper' to people without a lot of sailboat experience who wanted to charter a sailboat around the Keys. I wasn't licensed, so I couldn't be signed on as the skipper of the boat, but the charter company listed me as a deckhand for hire, and I would then join people on the sailboats they chartered and make sure they knew what they were doing. The charter company saw me as cheap insurance to protect their boats, as they knew I'd keep the charter folks from running aground or damaging the boat, as was common on direct charters to people with minimal sailing skills.

In addition to the charter work, I was also on the radar of the Singleton Shrimp Company, a large shrimp fishing operation working out of the Florida Keys, the Gulf of Mexico, and other areas. I'd heard plans that the company wanted to move a fleet of its trawlers down to the coast of South America and would soon be looking for American skippers to help round out the crews. As the boats were American-registered vessels, they'd need an American skipper on the outgoing manifest. I let it be known that I was available, asked to be considered, and forgot about it after a few weeks.

I was sleeping on my boat one afternoon after an all-night bender and heard a knocking on the bow of my boat. That's how most people greet you when you live on a boat. They either knock on the hull, or shout for you to see if you're aboard. I stuck my sleepy head up through the front hatch. A friend of mine from the marina was kneeling on the dock, about to knock on my hull again.

"What's up?" I asked.

"A guy from Singleton's is looking for you. They need another skipper."

"Cool. How do I get ahold of him?"

"He'll be around in a few minutes. He's in Gabe's office right now."

"Thanks, man. Appreciate the heads-up."

I popped below, pulled on a shirt, put on my flip-flops, and hopped on deck. As I was leaving my boat, I saw a man walking toward me. He looked up at me and nodded and continued toward me. I assumed he was the guy from the shrimp company, and I was correct.

"Kelly Harriger?" he asked, holding out his hand.

"That's me," I replied.

"How would you like to help deliver a trawler to Guyana?"

"That sounds like fun. When do you need me?"

"In about half an hour."

I wasn't prepared for that.

"Uh. In half an hour? Is this for a meeting?"

"No. We depart as soon as your paperwork is done. We leave today."

There I was, still stoned and a bit hungover, being asked if I wanted to leave for South America on a shrimp trawler in about an hour.

"Sure! Why not?"

I was an agreeable lad and rarely thought about my life beyond the next ten minutes.

After discussing where to meet, he departed, and I went back on my boat to grab some clothes for the trip. I wouldn't need much other than my usual garb. I looked in my laundry bag, saw three pairs of shorts and some t-shirts, so I grabbed those and my passport, closed the boat, told the dockmaster I'd be gone for a few weeks, and headed for the shrimp boat docks on Stock Island. I was on my way to South America. I took no weed or coke—a strict rule with Singleton—and I was happy that I'd be able to sober up for a few weeks.

Once I arrived at the docks, I learned that there would be ten shrimp trawlers in the fleet, and that we'd be crossing first into the Bahamas, skirting the southern edge of the archipelago, and then turning south through the strait between the Dominican Republic and Puerto Rico.

From that point, we'd take a course south-southwest toward Trinidad and Tobago, and continue down the coast until we reached Georgetown, Guyana, on the northern coast of South America. Each trawler would have one Guyanese crew member and one American crew member, who'd be listed on the manifest as the captain. I would be the captain on the trawler to which I was assigned, but as I'd never operated a 100-foot shrimp trawler before, my crewmate who did have experience—a Guyanese national of Indian descent—would be responsible for docking and disembarking anytime we were in port. My crew member's name was Ramesh Persaud, an easygoing fellow about thirty years old. We chatted a bit when introduced and quickly boarded the boat with the last manifest, an official document from US Customs that had me listed as "Master and Commander" of a 100-ton seagoing vessel, departing the port of Miami and bound for Guyana, S.A.

Cool shit, I thought. Master and Commander. I liked that title.

And just like that, after months of substance abuse and listlessly wondering what I was going to do with my life, I was on my way to South America on a fishing trawler.

The trip to Guyana was a great ocean-going adventure, a rollicking good time on the high seas. We were at sea for almost two weeks, under power the entire time with no stops. We didn't run at full power, as we were not scheduled to stop anywhere for fuel and had to make the entire voyage with the diesel fuel in our tanks upon departure. It was extraordinary to be back at sea, and I fell into my 'at sea' groove almost immediately. Ramesh seemed to love the sea as much as I did, and we talked about our love of the ocean on several occasions. He was part of a very large East Indian presence in Guyana, and people of Indian descent make up about 40% of the country's population, most having arrived as plantation workers in the 19th century.

Ramesh didn't like to cook, and when he found out that I did, he asked if I'd mind taking over as cook for the trip, and in return, he'd keep the galley clean and the pantry stocked, rather than sharing both duties as we'd originally planned. Shrimp trawlers have huge holds for ice, and each trawler had been loaded with a fair supply to keep things fresh on the trip. Although I wasn't getting paid very much for this trip—$135 and a return ticket home—the shrimp company traditionally spared no expense when it came to groceries, knowing that a well-fed crew was a happy crew. I went below and checked out the supplies, which Ramesh had been responsible for stocking before the trip. The man knew how to eat well, and I would have lots to work with. In the hold were all sorts of exotic cured meats, cheeses, fresh vegetables and fruits, and bags of frozen jumbo shrimp, as well as squid and mahi-mahi filets. Looking over our supplies, I was happy I'd ended up with Ramesh as a crewmate.

The trip was fun and relaxing, and generally uneventful. We never encountered any major storms and only dealt with a few short squalls that hit quickly and dissipated just as quickly. The only time we saw land was while passing through the straits between the Dominican Republic and Puerto Rico, when we sailed within about fifteen miles of the US territory. The trip was the longest continuous trip I'd made to date without making landfall, and I developed sea legs rather quickly, adapting to the boat's size and movement as it moved through the sea. Every boat had a different movement, caused by the hull size and shape, speed through the water, and the sea conditions. No two boats ever felt quite the same, and a trawler had a distinctly different movement pattern than a small 40-foot sailboat.

For the entire trip, we worked in six-hour watches. Six hours at the helm, and six hours sleeping or doing anything you wanted. My watches were from early morning until noon and six o'clock until midnight. During the days, we'd chat with the other trawlers spread out over roughly half a mile, two abreast and about a quarter mile apart. We ran on autopilot most of the time and had to make very minor adjustments from time to time to avoid converging courses and slight shifts caused by wind and current. During the afternoons, I'd often go out on the back deck while the ship was running on autopilot and climb up into the trawler rigging. I had to be very careful not to fall overboard, as Ramesh was usually sleeping, and the ship would just keep going if I fell overboard. The other trawlers were usually more than a quarter mile apart from us, and someone would have to be watching another trawler closely to witness someone falling overboard. I knew this and climbed carefully. Any mistake could mean my life.

Most trawlers were designed with a large steel structure in the center of the boat, known as a mast, and there were two long arms known as outriggers that could be lowered to each side to drag the nets that caught the shrimp. I stayed off the outriggers, because they were a bit looser than the main mast to which they were attached. From the top of the mast, I took a lot of photos of the cobalt blue sea below me. I watched dolphins join us, swimming in our wake as well as jumping near the bow. I turned my face to the sun and felt the sea breeze in my hair. I was miles from land, in the middle of the sea, and I felt at home like no other place on the planet. I was also amazed that I felt no withdrawal from alcohol or cocaine. It was as if I'd never done either before. I'd been using both heavily for months, and simply stepped onto the boat, set out to sea, and instantly felt refreshed and alive by the ocean. No headache, no listlessness, no withdrawal of any sort. The sea was my savior, and I realized that it was one of the few places where I truly loved to spend my time.

Looking back at that time in my life, I now realize that I loved the ocean because it separated me from the bad things in my life. It stripped away all the daily bullshit and reduced my life down to a simple set of tasks with a singular focus. It was good for me to be at sea, because it removed so many bad options for me and protected me from myself. But my love for the ocean went beyond this, I knew. It was also sheer magic, something otherworldly and special that so few people really had a chance to experience. Being at sea in a small boat, away from the comforts of land, in a world constantly in motion, was a singular experience that I couldn't repeat anywhere else, or so I thought at the time. I've since learned to find that solace and focus in the outdoors, mountains, or alone in the high country. It's necessary for a healthy soul.

After our two weeks at sea, we made ready for landfall in Georgetown, Guyana, SA. We landed at a commercial dock close to the city, after motoring inland about a mile on a wide, muddy river. Once all the trawlers were docked and secured, we called Customs and went back to the boats to wait. We were told that we'd be taken by car into the heart of Georgetown to the customs office for clearance and then return to the trawlers for an on-board inspection by government officials. During the trip, Ramesh had made a point of telling me not to use all the good cheese, as he needed it for "gifts." I was about to find out who those gifts were intended for, and it wasn't his family, as I'd first suspected. After being at the dock for about an hour, a representative of the Singleton Shrimp Company met us on the dock, led us to several cars, and we drove off the dock into the heart of Georgetown.

What happened next is an image that still lives vividly in my memories. When we arrived at the Customs office, we drove into a small square surrounded by two-story buildings with a balcony all around the top floor, overlooking the square. Several people inside the square stopped what they were doing to watch ten white men crawl out of some Toyota vans. We looked around, and the square was almost empty. We went into the Customs office, and within twenty minutes were cleared for entry and had our passports stamped. The shrimp company was very organized and had worked out any details in advance. All we had to do was show up and go through the paces.

We exited the building and headed for the vans. When we entered the building, there were fewer than ten people in the square. When we opened the door to return to the vans, about twenty minutes after arriving, the square had filled up completely, with hundreds of people. We were stunned and alarmed as well. People were standing two deep on the balcony that encircled the square, and easily more than one hundred people standing in the square, all looking at us. We stopped by the steps of the Customs office. One of the guys turned to our hosts.

"Is everything okay? Is it safe?"

The staffer from the shrimp company laughed.

"Yeah, you're just an oddity. They don't see things like this every day."

"Where'd they come from?" I asked.

He waved his hand in a broad arc. "Everywhere. You'll be okay."

We got back into the vans, and the crowd moved closer. I was nervous, but nobody looked dangerous. The crowd seemed to be composed of middle-aged to older women, and lots of children and teens. Grown men made up a very small part of the crowd. Nobody was smiling, however, and it made me uncomfortable. They may have been curious, but they didn't seem that friendly.

"Why do they look like that?" I asked. "They aren't saying anything. They even look a bit angry."

The man from the shrimp company turned around in his seat, looked at us in the passenger seats, and then nodded back toward the crowd encircling us.

"It's been five years since the Jonestown massacre, but it's still fresh in their minds. You're Americans, and they associate Americans with trouble. Americans aren't liked down here right now. We know it was an isolated incident, but it's still fresh in their minds, and to them, any American is a bad American. We simply must operate around that fact. Even elements in the government whom we work with are anti-American, although they're smart enough to know they can make money working with us."

That made sense. Once the vans were in gear and moving, the crowd parted to let us pass, but it was an unnerving experience. I made a note to keep my distance and ramp up my situational awareness for the remainder of the stay in Georgetown. It was a decision I'd be reminded of almost immediately after our return to the docks.

While we were gone, the boats had been put under armed guard to keep people from raiding them. Even though the trawlers were tied up on a commercial wharf, there were locals everywhere, looking for any opportunity to jump aboard and take what they could. As I returned to my trawler, I encountered a young man with dark skin and deep green eyes. I couldn't guess his ancestry, but if I were to guess, I'd guess he was a blend of many cultures and backgrounds. I'd been told by the man from Singleton's that the dock had a contract with guards who all belonged to a local Nation of Islam group. I tried to strike up a conversation with him, but he stared straight ahead, ignoring me.

I reached out my hand to introduce myself. "Hello. I'm Kelly," I said.

He turned to me, and his eyes burned through me.

"I don't like you or your people. You are a white, blue-eyed devil. The world will not know peace while it is run by white, blue-eyed devils."

This wasn't the greeting I was expecting. I tried to press on, but he cut me off. "We cannot be friends. I am here to guard your boat. Nothing else."

I stopped trying and turned to get back on the boat. Knowing that this guy was here to protect me made me a bit nervous. I finally accepted that he wasn't here to protect me and simply saw the boat and its contents as the only thing that needed his protection. If the chips were down and he had to defend me, I was certain he would turn away. I'd never experienced anything like this before, and it made me very uncomfortable. There was no reaching that guy.

Customs finally arrived for the trawler inspection, and I immediately learned why Ramesh had asked me to save some of the good cheese. As soon as our Customs official boarded the boat, he walked right to the galley and opened the icebox. He pulled out three large wheels of Gruyère cheese and two large bricks of Romano and Parmesan. He turned to us, standing behind him, and held them up.

"I may have these, right?" He was nodding yes.

Ramesh nodded, "Of course."

The customs officer continued to dig around the galley, pulling out boxes of crackers, cookies, and other treats, which he piled on the counter. When he was done, he nodded toward the items, now piled up beside his cheese.

"And these too? I may have these as well?"

"Of course," said Ramesh, nodding again.

"Okay! Let's look around."

It was immediately clear that the customs officer was done with the inspection. He showed absolutely no interest in anything else on the trawler and didn't even bother to inspect the hold or the large ice storage area, where Ramesh had hidden other food items from Customs. After less than a minute, after one pass around the top deck, the customs officer was done.

"Okay, you are cleared," he said. He walked back into the galley, pointed at his haul from our boat, and asked if we had a bag or box. Ramesh pulled a brown paper bag from a drawer and loaded it for the customs officer. That was it. We were cleared. As soon as he was off the boat, I turned to Ramesh.

"That's it? It seemed like he was mostly after a bribe. He didn't even inspect the boat."

"We have no big dairy industry here to speak of. What we do have is not very large or very productive. Good, aged cheeses are a real delicacy, even better than a money bribe. Whenever a boat docks here, they always go for the cheeses."

I nodded toward the back of the trawler.

"How'd you know he wouldn't search the ice box?"

"He already had what he wanted. He wasn't greedy. He's going to get more stuff off each boat. He'll go home with lots of good stuff and maybe share some with his staff."

We learned that the Singleton company didn't want to pay for hotels, and we were expected to sleep on the boats until the following day, when we'd be given our tickets home. Ramesh and all the other Guyanese crew would be returning to their homes and families, but the American crew members would be sleeping one more night in the shrimp boats on the dock. We all went out to some local bars that night, and we must have looked like easy targets to the locals, because we were swarmed by street-level drug dealers and prostitutes everywhere we went. I grew bored and tired and just wanted to get some sleep. I took a cab back to the docks and found the same armed guard I'd met earlier, the one who called me a white, blue-eyed devil, still guarding the boat. I greeted him, and he nodded but said nothing. I decided against trying to engage him in any more conversation. I made sure all the cabin doors were locked tightly and even grabbed a large chef's knife from the galley and kept it by my side all night.

The next morning, we gathered on the dock around 9 A.M., and we were driven to the airport to catch our flight back to Miami. Within thirty minutes after takeoff, we were landing again in Trinidad, as there'd been some sort of issue with the jetliner. We were ushered off the airplane and into a lobby. After checking with the flight crew and airline personnel, we learned that our next flight to Miami wouldn't be for another twenty-four hours. Distraught, we all walked to a corner of the main airport lobby and plopped down in the seats.

"What are we going to do?" I asked. The airline had already said they were not paying for hotel rooms.

"We just wait and go tomorrow," said Larry, the leader of our American group. He'd been designated the leader by the Singleton company, as he was our lead navigator.

"Where will we sleep?"

He pointed at the terrazzo floor. "Right here, I guess."

So that's what we did. None of us had enough money for a hotel room, and if anyone did, they weren't offering that information, so we threw down our duffel bags and prepared to camp out right in the airport. Later that evening, a man walked by and asked us what we were doing. He was Australian and in Trinidad on business, he told us. We explained our situation.

"Well, no need to sleep on the floor," he said. He opened his wallet and pulled out a $50 bill, USD. He handed it to us. "Go get a hotel room on me."

We were surprised.

"How can we pay you back?" I asked.

"Well, here's my card. You can pay me if you want to. If you don't, you don't. I'll leave that up to you lads."

"We really appreciate it. You didn't have to do that."

"Well, I like Yanks," he said. "Always get along with the Yanks, and you lads seem like good guys. Enjoy!" And off he went.

We had enough money now to get a room where we all could crash, take a shower, and get a decent night's sleep that wouldn't involve sleeping on a terrazzo floor. After a somewhat heated argument, we decided the best thing to do with the $50 was to get drunk, so we went to the airport lounge where we each had a few cocktails, and then we went back to our corner of the airport and slept through until the following morning, when we finally got our flight squared away. Later that day, we took off for Miami and then caught our Air Sunshine flight back to Key West. It was another great adventure on the high seas, but now I was right back where I shouldn't be, and things were about to get worse for me.

TWELVE

LAST GASP

Upon my return, I quickly fell back into my daily drinking and drug use. Without a job or any focus, there wasn't much else to do other than go sailing and snorkeling out on the reefs, which I did regularly, sometimes even alone. In the bars, I often met women on vacation, and once they learned I had a sailboat, they'd ask to go sailing. I always enjoyed these encounters, and in most cases, I ended up taking two or three friends on a sail to the reef, where we swam and snorkeled. I enjoyed playing the carefree local guy with the sailboat, and they loved hearing my stories. They were enjoying an experience not available to most tourists, and I enjoyed being the host. These interactions were mostly platonic, and I simply enjoyed being in the company of several fun, adventurous women. After the sail, they'd take me to dinner and buy me drinks, get some photos, and everyone had a great time. I thought about turning this activity into a small business, but to do so would require me to get a basic captain's license that would allow me to carry up to six paying passengers (a six-pack license, as it was called), and I wasn't sure I'd be eligible with my arrest record, so I passed on that idea.

Over the next few months, I started to recognize some bad thoughts creeping into my thinking. I'd never been one to drink or do drugs to cope with things. I drank to have fun, always. I was never a morose or depressed drunk. But as my drinking and drug use increased, it began to affect my mental well-being. I didn't drink because I was feeling down, but once I got drunk or high, I began to feel very depressed, and I suspected that I was experiencing some cognitive dissonance about my situation. In a nutshell, I had no job, no purpose, no goals, and no motivation to change things. My drinking and drug use were collapsing my world, reducing it to the same depressing patterns every day, and I didn't have the will to change it, so I increased the dosages of everything. The worst thing about this situation was that I had plenty of money, and I could have just left the Keys and started over somewhere. But I just wasn't ready to do that yet. I hadn't hit rock bottom, and sometimes you just must hit rock bottom to know when it's time to make a change.

On one of my trips to Miami to pick up more coke, Garry mentioned that he would be leaving town on a trip and would be gone for several days. He told me I could come up to stay in Miami while he was gone, and when he returned, he'd get me more coke. He'd since moved from his condo in Coconut Grove to a high-rise tower that had just been built, and had a luxury suite on the 17th floor, overlooking the Atlantic Ocean to the left from the balcony, and greater Miami to the south. I'd been there once before, and it sounded like a nice break from my current situation. I flew up a day before his trip, met some new woman he was dating, and he was off to the airport with her. I didn't know what had happened to Sarah, and didn't ask, but I suspect she'd finally just decided to move out and move on.

Garry had mentioned that the condo was another one of Luis's purchases. In fact, Luis had purchased three entire floors of the new tower, and they were all empty, save for Garry's. He also told me that many of Luis's upper-level partners had also purchased units in the building, sometimes buying entire floors, like Luis. I got the impression that most of the building was owned by drug lords looking to put their laundered cash into real estate. I walked out onto the balcony, leaned out, and looked around, and saw no signs of life. I went to the basement on the elevator and saw one car. In the outside parking lot, there was an old Corolla, which I guessed belonged to the single security guard in the lobby. I walked the halls on several floors and didn't see a sign of life in the entire complex. I was starting to think I was the only person in the entire building. It certainly looked like it. It was an eerie feeling.

I returned to Garry's apartment and turned on the TV. I set it on MTV, where it stayed for the next three days, around the clock. Garry had left me a quarter ounce of coke—about seven grams—just for personal use, so I cut out a few lines and got started. It was pure, as usual, and I didn't need to make long rails to get a good buzz. I didn't know the area and had no desire to go outside and walk around a strange neighborhood, so I just figured I'd stay indoors, watch TV, read some books I brought, and unwind for three days. That might have worked out just fine if I hadn't been sitting alone with seven grams of coke, all to myself. Before those three days were over, I would snort all seven grams of that coke while barely eating anything of substance.

The first day seemed fun and a bit decadent. I felt like a bad boy, snorting coke in a Miami high-rise overlooking the ocean, standing on the balcony in a bathrobe, wiping my nose a lot while MTV blasted in the background. Michael Jackson's mega-selling album "Thriller" had been released the previous year and was still getting heavy coverage everywhere. The first day, I found myself lying on the couch, watching TV, and day-dreaming a lot. Because I had what felt like an unlimited supply of coke at my disposal, I didn't feel any pressing need to do a lot. I knew I wouldn't be running out of it for a few days. I would feel exhausted from time to time, but the coke prevented me from falling asleep, and by the end of the first day, I was already in zombie mode, having done two grams over the course of the day. There was virtually no food in the refrigerator, as Garry was a fan of take-out meals and rarely cooked anything himself. I found a box of cookies, but they seemed tasteless, and I only ate one. I found myself shuffling around the condo aimlessly, forgetting why I was going into other rooms. I walked out to the balcony and felt strangely drawn to the railing. As I approached, I found myself wondering what it would be like to fly. The appearance of that thought scared me enough to step away from the balcony and go back inside. This would become a recurring event over the next two days, with the thoughts of jumping becoming stronger and stronger.

Late in the first day, I backed off on the lines for a few hours and found myself drifting off to sleep. It didn't last long, but it was just enough to refresh me and let me feel like I was back in control of my thoughts. I went back to the couch and collapsed into the cushions and continued to watch MTV until daybreak. I made some Cuban coffee and some toast but never touched the toast. The smell of food made my stomach turn, but the coffee tasted great. Back in the living room, I cut out a few more lines and started the second day.

By noon, I'd snorted most of the third gram and was flying high. I had no recollection of time passing, and I was back in zombie mode, staring blankly at walls for great lengths of time without realizing what I was doing, and then suddenly becoming aware of it and finding myself feeling puzzled by how much time had slipped by. And throughout it all, I heard the constant droning of MTV videos playing in the background, a soundtrack to my madness. I was vaguely aware of my condition, but if I could think about my condition, I felt I had some measure of control over myself. I recall thinking that I'd be okay as long as I continued to think about what I was doing. I told myself that I should slow down and go for a walk, but that idea never materialized. I walked around the hallways of the 17th floor, wondering if there was a gym I could use, but found nothing. I went to the lobby and asked the security guard if there was a gym in the building. He stared at me, concern on his face.

"Are you okay, sir?" he asked. He looked worried.

"Sure! I'm fine. Just checking to see if you had a gym in the building."

"No. No gym. I'm sorry," he said. "Are you sure you're okay?"

I waved him off. "I'm fine. Thanks."

I took the elevator back to the 17th floor and walked to the bathroom, where I saw myself in a mirror. I immediately understood the guard's concern. I looked frightening. I even startled myself. I haven't shaved in a few days, and my hair—which was long then—was sticking out wildly in every direction. And my eyes! My eyes were wide open and burning holes through everything. I found myself recoiling from my own image. The guy in the mirror looked crazy. I didn't feel crazy, but that guy in the mirror certainly looked crazy. It startled me enough to take a shower and shave in the hope of taming the beast in the mirror.

I stood in front of the mirror after showering and shaving. I looked a bit more respectable and a lot less crazy, but those eyes were still wide open. I stared at the person in the mirror for several minutes, and as the time passed, I grew confused. The eye contact with the stranger in the mirror frightened me. I didn't know that guy, and I didn't want to be him, or even be associated with him. As I stood there, I realized for the first time in my life that we have carefully constructed images of ourselves that we protect at all costs, even if they're not in alignment with reality. Standing in front of that mirror, I realized that the drugs had stripped away any illusions I had about myself, and I was seeing who I really was for the very first time in my life. I didn't like what I was seeing, but I was fascinated by the process that had taken me there. At that point, my instincts for self-preservation were taking a back seat to my desire to learn more about this process and how far I could take it.

I walked back to the couch, my head filled with some of the most intrusive thoughts I'd ever experienced. I felt overcome by them, and I was seeing myself in a new light, through a new pair of eyes that I didn't realize even existed until that moment. I sat down on the couch, perched on the edge, and stared out through the sliding glass door to the balcony. I felt I'd just started a journey into my own mind, and I was so fascinated with continuing that I never considered the dangers I would encounter along the way.

With fresh resolve, I dumped about an entire gram of coke onto the table and cut it into clean, neat lines, side by side. I immediately did two of them and lay back on the couch as the rush hit my brain. The ceiling opened above me, revealing the sky, and my head was filled with music. I lay on my back, staring into the heavens, taking slow, deep breaths even though my heart was racing and approaching redline. Using just thoughts, I attempted to slow my heart rate, and after a few minutes of deep meditation, it began to slow, and I felt my body relax. At that moment, I felt I was on to something big. I didn't know what, but it felt important, like I'd made a breakthrough in mind-body control. It was just the drugs talking, but I didn't know that.

Time lost its meaning, and I lost sense of time. All moments in time seemed to exist simultaneously, and I found myself recalling experiences throughout my life, multiple experiences, all at the same time, as though the past had compressed with my present, and all the moments now existed together. It seemed like a great time to do a few more lines, so I did.

The remainder of the day, hour by hour, was just a repeat of the previous hour. I'd lost all sense of time and was doing a few lines of coke every hour, staring at the TV, walking around the room, and fighting off the urge to go back out on the balcony. The balcony became a pressing issue, and I kept finding myself walking toward the glass sliding doors, literally shouting "NO!" out loud to myself to prevent myself from opening the door and going onto the balcony. To this day, I don't understand what was drawing me there or making me think about jumping. I wasn't feeling suicidal, and I certainly wanted to live, yet I couldn't stop thinking about what it would feel like to just float off the balcony and head for the ground. It was a powerful draw, and I had no idea where it was coming from. It was as if there was another person within me, trying to convince me to act against my own wishes. This became my primary concern as I snorted my way into the third day.

By the evening of the second day, I knew I wanted to try to sleep and get some rest, so I decided to repeat what I'd done the previous day. I stopped doing coke for a few hours, made some coffee, which, in retrospect, seemed a bit crazy. Imagine being so high on cocaine that you drink Cuban espresso coffee to come down from your high. It's laughable now, but I think the caffeine was a more familiar drug, and my body was just hanging on for dear life. I don't know that it reduced my high, but it altered it enough that I felt different. After some coffee, I took a long shower, close to an hour. There was a seemingly endless supply of hot water, not something I was used to, and I took advantage of it. The long shower and the coffee worked their magic, and I felt like a new man. The only problem was that I'd been doing coke for two days straight, and even though my high was slightly blunted by the shower and coffee, it was still lurking close by, ready to return in an instant. I might have slept a few hours, but I don't remember much. I do remember feeling a bit better around midnight, and rather than continue to come down, I did the opposite and returned to the coffee table to snort up two more lines.

I was really rolling by then. It took just two lines to bring my high right back online, full force, and with it the crushing doubts, worries, speculations, deep thoughts, cognitive dissonance, and paranoia that had been swirling around my brain for the past few days. Whatever was driving me to keep doing coke had far more power over me than my rational side. Whatever was driving me seemed to be taking on a separate personality within me, and I found myself at war with myself. Part of me worked for control and self-preservation, and another part of me was hell-bent on tearing down any semblance of sanity and reason. It was that latter part of me that kept urging me toward the balcony, and by the third day, I was fighting off this urge almost every hour.

I could not even look at the balcony door without thinking about opening it, walking through, and jumping. It was a very powerful urge, and I could barely control it. I had to keep talking to myself, sometimes out loud, saying, "It will kill you. Don't do it. It will kill you." It's difficult for me to express this to someone who'd never been in that situation, but anyone who'd been deeply into drugs has no doubt experienced some version of this frightening encounter with our darker side. I'm now convinced that it exists even in the best of people, but most live their lives in such a manner as to never encounter it. But there are things you can do to unlock this beast, and I understand now why not all survive this experience.

I remember at one point during the third day, when I was well into the sixth gram of coke, I felt that I needed to overcome whatever it was that kept driving me toward the balcony. I stood in the center of the living room and took several long, deep breaths. I walked to the balcony door and opened it. I stepped onto the balcony, but stood by the door, once again gathering my thoughts. I took several deeper breaths and stepped up to the balcony. For a moment, everything felt beautiful. The sun warmed my face, the breeze blew through my hair, and the ocean air felt good in my lungs. I looked over the balcony and down to the parking lot below. Seventeen stories were a long way down. I closed my eyes and took another deep breath. Everything felt so beautiful, and right at the tail end of that thought, I suddenly was hit with the urge to jump over the balcony. It was as though another person had entered my thoughts and taken them over by force. I recoiled in horror, collapsing to the floor of the balcony and curling into a fetal position. I kept saying, "No, no, no. Go away." There was another presence, and it had just exposed itself as an evil one, bent on my destruction. Up until that point, I thought it was just an internal struggle caused by the drugs. It well may have been, but what I felt at that moment was the literal presence of another being, something not me, and it horrified me. I remained curled up in a fetal position for a long time, close to an hour, just making certain that I was in control before moving again. When

I finally felt a sense of control, I crawled on my hands and knees back into the living room and locked the balcony door behind me.

Once inside, I stood up and walked back to the couch. MTV was still going strong. I held out my hand, and it was steady as a rock, which surprised me. I was filled with a sense of relief and took a few deep, slow breaths to calm myself. Once I felt as though I had control, I snorted two more lines of coke. I really didn't know when to quit. It had become as natural as breathing.

For the remainder of that day, I just stayed on the couch and snorted a few lines every hour. I was a total zombie, staring into space or at a blank wall, with no sense of time or awareness. Late in the afternoon, I was jolted out of my haze by the ringing of the telephone, the first time it had rung since Garry left three days earlier. It rang several times before I realized I was the only one in the house, and that I should probably answer it.

It was Garry.

"Hey! How's it going?"

"I'm great. How about you?"

"Doing great! Hey, just letting you know I'll be back around seven o'clock. I'll have some stuff for you to take back with you."

"Sounds great! I'll see you then," I said. We made some more small talk, then hung up.

I looked at the clock. It was about 3 P.M. I had four hours to try to sober up a bit, so I snorted some more coke. And a bit later, two more lines. Before Garry walked through the door, I'd snorted the last of the quarter ounce he'd left for me three days earlier. I was as high as I'd ever been, and barely in control of myself. That's not to say that I couldn't present a version of myself to others that appeared to be in control, because that's exactly what I did when he arrived.

As soon as I heard Garry's key in the lock, I flipped a switch and went into my "normal" mode. I know it wasn't totally effective, but it was a marked difference from the coked-up zombie I'd been just an hour earlier.

I stood up from the couch and turned around. Garry walked in, locked the door behind him, and turned around. He laughed, then shook his head.

"You look like shit," he said with a grin. "Did you get outside at all?"

"No, I just stayed in. Watched some TV and read books."

"For three days? Damn." He looked at the coffee table. "Okay, now I see why. Jesus, you did all that by yourself?"

"Yes," I said. "Probably should have saved some, I guess."

"Well, it was for you. You were free to do whatever you wanted with it. But holy shit. All of it? Damn."

I shrugged. I suddenly felt exhausted, both mentally and physically, and I just wanted to be home, sound asleep on my boat, back in my comfort zone.

"The last flight out is 8:45," I told him. "I'd like to try to make that one if possible. If you have my stuff."

He opened his luggage, pulled out his shaving kit, and pulled three ounces of coke from inside. He slapped it to my chest and held it there until I took it.

"You're welcome to stay tonight and catch a morning flight if you'd like," he said.

I sighed and took a deep breath. "I'd really like to get back tonight. I'm just beat, and this way I can just sleep in tomorrow."

"Be my guest," he said.

I wasn't certain I was in any shape to be in public, but by then I didn't care. I had tunnel vision, and I was tired. I just wanted to be home and sleeping on the boat. It was my only safe spot, the one place I felt completely and totally comfortable.

Garry called me a cab while I took a large plastic freezer bag from the counter, packed the three ounces inside, and tucked them into the front of my underwear, then pushed them down a bit to be less conspicuous.

"I'm all set," I said.

Garry glared at me.

"Stop doing that," he said.

"Doing what?"

"That thing with your arms. You're moving your arms around and scratching them too much. What the hell?"

I wasn't aware of anything out of the ordinary until he brought it to my attention. I looked at what I was doing, and it surprised me. I was holding my arms across my chest and clawing and scratching at my elbows. I wasn't aware that I was doing it and didn't even know why I was doing it.

"Don't be doing that in public," he said. "You'll draw attention to yourself. It looks weird, like you're drugged or something."

"I am drugged, or something," I said.

"In this case, not funny. You're about to walk through Miami International carrying three ounces of coke. You most definitely do not want to draw attention to yourself."

He was right. I was about to go out among people for the first time in three days, coked out of my brains, and I needed to get my shit together quickly.

"Okay," I told him. "I got this. I'm good."

"You're still welcome to spend the night and go tomorrow."

"No, I want to go now. I just want to be home."

"I'm not going to argue with you. You're a grown man. You can make your own decisions."

The cab would be arriving shortly, so I said goodbye and headed down to the lobby to catch my cab. It arrived shortly after I stepped outside, and I hopped in and headed to the airport. I felt calm but noticed I was starting to sweat profusely. It wasn't particularly warm, but I was sweating like it was 90 degrees with 100% humidity. I kept wiping my forehead with my hands. The cab driver noticed and handed me a box of tissues. I took several and thanked him.

I arrived at the airport, paid the driver, and walked into the terminal. The rush of humanity all around me was startling. After three days of isolation and heavy drug use, I was suddenly surrounded by people and found my paranoia meter suddenly going to redline. I could feel the sweat running down my back, down my chest, and off my forehead, and I felt that everyone was looking at me. I looked overhead at the lighted board with the flights and gates, found my departure gate, and headed in that direction. It was a long walk, and the corridors were crowded. I was dressed in flip-flops, some well-worn loose-fitting khaki trousers, and an old Hawaiian shirt worn open over a dark t-shirt, which was now soaked in sweat. Considering that I was carrying three ounces of coke, it might have been in my best interest to dress differently, but it was too late for that. Just another few hundred yards to my gate, and I'd be seated on a flight back to the Keys, and home.

The crowds in the corridor were dense, and although everyone on my side of the walkway was going in my direction, most were moving too slowly for me, and I began to walk around them, dodging others as I passed the slow movers. The closeness of the crowd was starting to get to me, and I felt claustrophobic.

Suddenly, out of the corner of my eye, I spotted a man in a suit with a clip-on badge attached to his lapel. As soon as I made eye contact, he held my gaze and started walking through the oncoming crowd toward me. I panicked and stopped, not knowing what to do next. My heart rate had already been way up, and now it was going through the roof. I felt a sense of doom, like my life was about to end, and I was powerless to stop it. I turned around, looking to go in another direction. As soon as I turned, I saw another man on the other side of the corridor moving toward me. He was dressed just like the first one, wearing a suit, with a badge attached to his lapel. They were closing in on me from both sides, and I had one option . . . turn and run. But where would I run to? I had no place to go. I was trapped. It was all over.

I remember thinking, "So this is how it ends."

I was on probation, and if caught with three ounces of cocaine, I was almost certainly looking at a prison sentence. I didn't know what to do. As they closed in, I suddenly felt a strange sense of relief, as though something very stressful was about to come to an end. As I prepared for my arrest, I felt my body relax and go limp, the stress gone.

But that relief was short-lived.

As they closed in, I stood still, closed my eyes, ready to accept my fate, at peace with my decision not to run.

"Excuse me, sir."

I opened my eyes, and the two men in suits with badges on their lapels stood before me. I was immediately confused. They didn't look like law enforcement at all. They looked like door-to-door salesmen in cheap thrift-store suits, and a bit goofy.

"Sir, may we have a minute of your time to talk to you about your life?" He pulled a book from a small satchel slung over his shoulder inside his cheap suit. He held the book in front of my face. On the cover of the book were the words BHAGAVAD GITA.

When they'd first walked up to me, I'd calmed myself and readied myself for an arrest. When I suddenly realized that these guys were the same people who normally ran around the airport in saffron robes with shaved heads, peddling Hindu scripture to the masses, I completely lost my shit . . .completely, totally, and violently.

I'd just spent the past three days getting coked out of my skull, and at that moment I was probably as tense and wound up as I'd ever been in my entire life. I was grinding my teeth, pawing at my elbows, sweating profusely, and imagining one bad thing after another happening to me as I tried to get home to safety. When I first accepted that I was about to be arrested, I had calmed myself and almost felt a sense of relief that this was all about to end. But upon realizing that I wasn't going to be arrested, and that I was simply being accosted by some out-of-uniform Hare Krishnas, I lost it.

I turned toward the one who'd held up the book to me. I turned violent.

"NO!" I screamed in his face. I pushed him backward with all my might, knocking him off his feet, and into the backs of several people passing by, knocking them down as well. I turned to the other man, who was frozen in his tracks with a horrified look on his face. I made some growling sound right in his face and pushed him in the chest with everything I could muster, and sent him flying backwards, also knocking down several people. I stood there for a few seconds, and then I panicked.

I'd just created a scene, and it was bound to attract attention most likely in the form of airport security, and possibly any law enforcement who might be in the airport. I didn't have any illusions what would happen to me if I were to be caught with three ounces of coke.

Once I realized what I'd done, I knew I had to get the hell out of there and get to my gate as quickly as possible. I put my head down and walked as fast as I could, fully expecting to have someone following me and trying to stop me. I paced with purpose for about one hundred yards and turned around. I didn't see anyone following me, although I saw some people around the area of the encounter still watching me as I walked away. I walked another fifty feet, and then turned into a waiting area, where I milled around with waiting passengers who were standing up to board their flight. I took off my Hawaiian shirt, folded it, and put in into my duffel bag. I walked to the edge of the long corridor and looked around a corner. Still nobody following me, but I was certain I'd probably been captured by a security camera, and it would just be a matter of time before someone was sent to look for me. I stood and looked down the corridor for another minute. Still nobody following me, so I walked around the corner into a rest room, found a stall, and sat down inside. I waited several minutes, and heard people coming and going, but nothing to alert me. I left the stall, walked to the sinks, rinsed my face with cold water, looked at myself in the mirror to compose myself, and walked back out into the corridor.

Everything seemed normal, and I breathed easier.

My gate was just a bit farther down the concourse, so I walked slowly toward it, with my boarding pass out. I checked in, took a seat, and within a few minutes I was on my flight and seated. Still nothing. I ordered a Miami Whammy, turned the little overhead AC nozzle directly on my face, and relaxed. A few minutes later the airliner moved away from the loading dock, and several minutes later we were cleared for takeoff. Less than an hour later I was on the ground in Key West and in a cab headed for Stock Island and Oceanside Marina. Once back on my boat, I stretched out on some boat cushions in the cockpit, stared at the sky, and fell into a very deep sleep, my first in almost four days.

I awoke late the next morning, still in my clothes. Some people were staring at me from the powerboat landing, but they were just tourists. I didn't feel too good, and my nerves were still buzzing, but I could tell I was coming down off my high and walked down the street for some breakfast. It was the first meal I'd eaten in several days, and it tasted great. As I ate, I realized that something had finally snapped, some line had been crossed, and there was no going back. I knew it was time to make some changes. I simply could not keep living that lifestyle and expect to have a long or happy life.

In the days immediately following my return, I decided that once I was done selling the cocaine in my possession, I was getting out of the cocaine business for good. I talked to my sellers, let them know they'd have to find another source, and unloaded everything I had, keeping none for myself this time around. I got Garry's money to him, pocketed my cut, and wiped my hands of the cocaine business. It was a clean departure. It would be years before I allowed myself to be around any cocaine, and even then, I found myself repulsed by the thought of doing it. I remember watching a movie where an actor did a line, and I could literally feel my own nose burn when he did it. I didn't realize it at the time, but I'd also destroyed the cilia in my nasal passages. Years later, while being checked for allergies and frequent sinus infections, a doctor had examined my nostrils and quietly asked me if I'd done any cocaine when I was younger. Apparently, it's easy to see the damage, and I've had sinus and nasal problems ever since.

I was done with cocaine at this point, but not drinking, nor my marijuana use. After quitting cocaine, I began to replace it with increased use of weed and booze. I sometimes look back at this period in my life and wonder how I managed to stay alive through it all, as I had several friends in the Keys die from substance abuse. I think one of the reasons I survived is because I was always a runner. Even in my heavy use days, I never stopped running, and I would drag myself out of bed with a terrible hangover to go running. I'm not sure if this alone saved my life, but I have no doubt that it helped a lot.

Without my drug business to support me, I knew I'd have to get to work at some point.

Several months after retiring from my cocaine business, I finally went to the bank, sat down with my safe deposit box, and counted my remaining money. I could finally see the bottom of the tray, and knew my money was about to run out. I was a big fan of Ernest Hemingway, and recalled a famous quote of his: "How do you go bankrupt? Two ways. Gradually, then suddenly." It was an accurate quote. While I had money, everything seemed fine, and I felt wealthy . . . right up until I didn't have money anymore. I took the last of the cash, a few thousand dollars, and closed out the safe deposit box. It was time to get a job.

I found some work at Oceanside Marina, working for a marine service center, and spent my days working on boats. I liked the job, and it paid okay, but I could feel my time in Key West coming to an end. I loved the place with all my heart and soul, but I knew if I stayed, I'd probably get into trouble again at some point. I was working again, but as soon as 5 P.M. rolled around, I was next door at the bar, drinking until I obliterated myself, and then I'd go back to my boat and fall asleep, only to repeat it the next day.

I had dinner with Greg one night, and he said he had to talk to me. He told me not to get mad at him. I knew what he was going to tell me.

"I think you should leave town," he said. "You're going to die if you stay here. I'm saying this as a friend. I don't want to see you destroy yourself. You have a lot going for you, but you're never going to know that or realize that if you stay here."

"I've thought about it," I said. I was surprised to hear myself say it, though.

"You should really think about it. I don't see you really returning to the work force or trying to build a career here. The lifestyle is too tempting for someone like you. You seem addicted to things that are bad for you."

"I'm addicted to sailing. I'm addicted to the ocean. What's wrong with that?"

"Nothing. There's nothing wrong with that. But you're also addicted to the lifestyle that you think goes with them. But you don't need that lifestyle to enjoy them."

"I can change that."

"I'm going to disagree with you there. I don't see you changing. I see a guy who can't let it go and is trying to hang onto something he should be letting go of for his own sake."

I knew in my heart that he was right, but I had a hard time admitting it to myself. "Where would I go?"

"If I were you, I'd go to where my family lives. Someplace you know, around people who know you. Those people know you as someone different, so they will expect you to be that person. Yeah, I know that's peer pressure, but it might be just what you need right now."

He could tell I wasn't ready to talk about the subject and backed off.

"Hey," he said. "Just putting that thought in your mind. It's your decision to make, but I think it would be a good one."

"I appreciate it. You aren't the only person who's suggested it. Pete and Barb said something like it the other night. Not as precisely as you, but I could tell where they were going with it."

"Think about it," he said, then tipped his beer to me. "Here's to the good times, no matter where we land."

I gave it some thought in the weeks ahead and knew I was probably heading in that direction, but I still hadn't made any final decisions. There was a part of me that felt connected to Key West; it was a part of my soul and spirit. I loved the place and the lifestyle, even without the smuggling trips, money and drugs that followed. It was just a beautiful place to live, and I still couldn't imagine living anywhere else.

I continued to work at my job, but I wasn't saving any money. I had fallen into a pattern of working all day and partying all night. But even I could see that things were starting to unravel at the seams. I stumbled out of the Full Moon Saloon one night, so drunk I could barely walk, to find that my motorcycle battery was dead (or so I thought at the time). My BMW had an electric starter without a kick starter, so the only way to start it with a dead battery was to start pushing it down the road as fast as you could with it in 2nd gear and the clutch held in, then jump on the bike and pop the clutch. I was drunk, and after a few tries, I apparently blacked out, fell over, and the bike landed on top of me. I remember leaving the bar and finding that my battery was dead, but I don't remember much after that until I woke up on my back with my motorcycle laying on top of me, and some woman screaming at me for being a drunk. Her boyfriend was trying to pull her away from me, and I remember him saying, "Let's get out of here. He'll think we did it. Let's go!" I was confused and had no idea how long I'd been laying there, but the boyfriend finally succeeding in pulling his girlfriend away, and I watched them hurry down the street.

I stayed on my back while I slowly gathered my senses and then managed to pull my legs out from under the bike, which weighed over 400 pounds. The bike had a roll bar around the cylinder heads, so I didn't have any real problem sliding my legs out from under it. I sat on the sidewalk for a moment when I suddenly noticed my wallet laying on the ground near the bike. I grabbed it and saw that all my money had been taken. I usually carried several hundred dollars cash, and it was gone. Someone had robbed me while I lay unconscious under the bike, and the behavior of the couple suddenly made sense. I stood up and walked around for a bit to clear my head and had a decision to make. Should I call the cops and take the risk of being arrested for public drunkenness? Or should I just call it a night?

As I've noted before, I wasn't a smart man. I was angry that I'd been robbed, and I walked back into the Full Moon and used the payphone to call the police to report a robbery. The police arrived and I walked the officer to where the bike was parked and explain that I'd been robbed. He asked what time, and I didn't know.

"You don't remember what time you were robbed?" he asked.

"It was shortly after I left the bar around 10 P.M."

He looked at his watch and made a face. "Sir, it's almost 1 A.M. What have you been doing for the past three hours? Why didn't you call me when this happened?"

I suddenly realized what a stupid thing I'd done, and my mind went into overdrive trying to come up with something coherent.

"I was passed out, I guess. My battery was dead, and I tried to push it to start it, and I guess I just got lightheaded and fell over. I came to and found my wallet empty beside me."

"Had you been drinking?"

"I'd had a few beers." That was a lie. I'd been drinking rum and had consumed at least five glasses. "I have asthma," I offered, as an afterthought.

He sighed deeply, shook his head, and put his hands on his hips.

"Here's what I can do. I can file a report of a theft, but I have no details. You can't provide any details. I suspect you were drunk, although you don't seem to be now, and you weren't operating a vehicle, so I can't do anything about that. If you want to continue, then I'll have to press you for more information, and I suspect you're not telling me the entire truth. Which direction would you like to go with this?"

I thought about it for a while and decided to cut my losses while I was ahead. "I guess I'll just head home," I said.

"That will be absolutely fine with me. Saves me trying to create some bullshit paperwork for something going nowhere. I'm not sure what happened here, but I hope you learned a lesson."

I thanked him for his time and then apologized for wasting it. One thing I always liked about the Key West police officers at that time was their willingness to look at situations in a reasonable manner. Going by the book on everything just created a lot of paperwork, and incidents like mine were more of a pain in the ass than a real problem, especially in a tourist town where they were commonplace.

"How are you going to get home?" he asked.

"I'm going to try to push-start the bike," I replied.

"I thought that's what made you pass out last time."

"I think I tried too many times and just got winded. It usually starts right up."

"Well, if it will help, I'll give you a push."

I went to turn on the key, but it wasn't in the ignition where it should have been. I reached into my front pocket and found the key. The bike wouldn't push-start earlier because I hadn't turned the ignition on. The officer was no fool. He watched me reach for the ignition, then watched me find the key in my pocket. He laughed and shook his head but said nothing. I'd been too drunk to remember my key earlier, and he knew it. He helped me push my bike down the alley, and it started on the first bump. I stopped, turned around, and thanked him again.

"Just get home safely. I don't want to see or hear from you again tonight."

I crossed the bridge to Stock Island, but the night air felt great, and I decided to go for a ride. Once off the island of Key West, I was in the jurisdiction of the Florida Highway Patrol. I knew they were rarely out late and didn't set speed traps in the middle of the night. Those troopers on duty were usually sitting near bars that late at night, watching for drunks and erratic drivers. I was feeling sober by then and thought a nice ride up the Keys would clear my head before going home for the night. Riding up the Keys at night was something I did on a regular basis. I loved the smell of the night air, and I could exceed the speed limit on the bridge without worrying about encountering a state trooper, as there was no place to park and set a speed trap. I also knew that the section of highway between Big Coppitt and Lower Sugarloaf was almost all bridge, with just a few small sections of the highway touching small pieces of land, which were mostly mangroves. It was in that section that I often drove way faster than I should have, although I usually did so sober. Tonight was different. I was frustrated and angry about being robbed and felt belligerent for reasons unknown. I was having an internal fight between my better instincts and my worse ones, and tonight I was giving free rein to my worse ones.

Once north of Big Coppitt Key, I opened the throttle and held it there until I was going over 100 mph. I'd driven that speed before, but never after drinking. I didn't care. I remember opening myself to whatever happened, and I held the throttle open. I didn't care about having an accident.

I didn't care about dying. As the air drag began to come into play, I leaned forward with my face low over the tachometer, and then, without even thinking, lifted my feet off the pegs and stretched my legs out on the seat behind me so that I was prone on my stomach, chest resting on the gas tank, flying down the highway at 100 mph. It wouldn't have taken much to knock the bike off balance—a stone, a branch, any little obstruction on the highway could have done it. I really didn't care. I held the throttle open and wondered how long I could maintain that speed until I chickened out or something happened. I was daring the Universe to take some action and force my hand in one direction or another. I honestly didn't care which direction. I would have been okay with death.

At 100 mph, the immediate area around you is a blur. You can't see any details. What happens at that speed is something I've always found interesting. At 100 mph, as the things near you turn to a blur, your focus—mainly around the outer periphery of your vision—notices things far away from you begin to drift by in slow motion. It's a fascinating sensation, and I remember seeing the lights of freighter ships miles out in the Gulfstream floating in the corner of my right eye, then fade from sight. The night air was cool, and smelled like seaweed and hibiscus, a strange scent. After a minute at full throttle, I backed off a bit and lowered my legs until my feet were back on the pegs. I held the grips tightly as I raised myself back up to a full sitting position, and I allowed the wind drag alone to slow me down to a safer 60 mph. When I reached Lower Sugarloaf, I pulled over to a small coral-covered side road and parked the bike. I took off my helmet and sat on the ground. I had tears in my eyes, but I didn't cry. I was too far gone for crying. I was lost. I finally realized it. I had no goal, no plans, no money, and no real ambition other than getting to a bar every day and getting wasted. My life was going nowhere, and although I lacked the balls to do something to myself, I'd put myself in a position to allow something to happen to me. I'd offered myself up to Death, but Death, apparently uninterested, turned me away. With no other choices, I knew I'd have to fix my problems on my own. I knew it was time to leave Key West and start over somewhere else.

I rode back to the marina at a safe pace, feeling exhausted and lost. I parked the bike on the dock, climbed onto the boat, and fell asleep. I didn't get up the next day and told my boss at the marine repair shop that I was sick and wouldn't be in that day. I slept on and off throughout the day and never left the boat until that evening. I sat in the cockpit and made my plans, which I would carry out with precision over the days to follow.

The first thing I had to do was lighten my load. Everything I owned in the world was on the boat. It wasn't much, but it was more than I could carry in the motorcycle's saddlebags or strapped to the carrier. I sold my guitars to the local guitar shop and packed up my typewriter and some books in a box and shipped them to my parent's house via UPS. I worked out a deal with the sailboat's original owner, who technically still owned the boat, as we'd never transferred the title, so that problem was quickly solved. I'd given up my apartment on Margaret Street months earlier when I moved to the marina full-time, so I had no issues with property. All I had left to do was say goodbye to a very small handful of close friends who'd stood by me through thick and thin, and it was time to go.

"I'm happy for you," said Greg. "It's the right move. You'll be glad you did this."

I wasn't so sure, but I knew it was the right thing to do at that moment.

Pete and Barb were next. I stopped by, we ate dinner together, smoked a joint, chatted a bit, listened to some jazz one last time, and I was on my way. I'd miss them.

I visited several other longtime friends, said my goodbyes, and I was ready to go.

I slept one more night on the boat and woke early. I'd packed up the motorcycle the day before, so it was ready to go when I woke up. I walked to the dock master's office to say goodbye to Gabe, walked to the shop to buy a coffee and a Danish, and sat on the dock to finish my breakfast.

And all too soon, it was time to leave.

I don't think I'd ever felt as sad as I did that morning. I was distraught to be leaving a place that I loved so much. I also knew by then that I had to leave and that I had no choice. Greg was right. If I stayed, I'd probably be dead within a year. I had no idea what awaited me, but I knew my parents were anxious to have me move home. They'd found out about my smuggling life and were worried for me. After my arrest, the local paper, The Key West Citizen, had run a story about our bust. One of my father's former officers had retired in the Keys and had read the article in the newspaper and had then clipped it out and sent it to my father. I had no idea how my parents had handled this news, but I knew them well enough to know they were worried about me, and I would be welcomed home to get a fresh start.

I started my motorcycle, pulled out of the marina one last time, and drove down Maloney Avenue toward US Highway 1, where I began my journey home. I stopped at the intersection, put on my turn signal, pulled onto the highway heading north, crossed the Boca Chica Channel bridge, and never once looked back.

EPILOGUE

I returned to Key West to visit my friends once more, a few years later in 1987. By then, I'd found a job in Philadelphia working at a photo agency, and I'd returned to college to get a degree in Communications with plans to get into advertising and marketing. Upon leaving Key West, I'd immediately stopped drinking and smoking, and experienced no withdrawal, either physical or emotional. I just walked away from weed and booze without a second thought and started a new life. With a new location came new motivation, and I never looked back.

After my brief return visit, I never returned to the Keys or Key West. I've always meant to, and I might someday just to see how much it has changed, but I have no desire to recapture any of that particular life. If I go back, it will be to look at it with a fresh set of eyes, but for now, I'm good. We had our time together, and I lived a life there that's impossible to forget. I have memories that will last a lifetime, and they remain vivid every time I replay them in my mind. If I never return, I'll be fine with the memories.

My friends scattered over the years, most drifting away from Key West. Pete and Barb moved to Miami shortly after I left and remain there to this day. Greg passed away several years ago from a medical condition, and I felt fortunate to have had the opportunity to talk by telephone just a few years earlier. He may have known something about his condition at the time, but he never let on and we had a great time catching up. I have been in touch with several other good friends from my life there, mostly through social media, which is how I stay current with what's going on in their lives.

Looking back, I have no regrets. What I did felt like the right thing to do at the time, and I was a young guy with some wild dreams I needed to fulfill. I knew what I was doing was illegal and did it anyway. I was willing to accept whatever the world threw at me without complaint, even if it meant some jail time. Quite simply, I moved there to live a dream of mine and live it to the fullest without regrets, and I believe I succeeded.

ABOUT THE AUTHOR

KELLY RYAN HARRIGER grew up in a military family that rarely stayed put for more than a few years at a time when he was young. His father was an Air Force base commander, and his mother a former Marine turned journalist. He spent much of his early life near the sea, first in Hawaii, and then in the Florida Keys, and developed a deep love of the ocean and boating during those formative years. He always dreamed of returning to the ocean, and upon leaving college in Texas, he returned to the Keys determined to make a life for himself while living the boating life and writing about it.

He partially succeeded at making that dream a reality, and eventually gave it up to return to college and move into the field of marketing and advertising, where he became a copywriter and editor with ad agencies and marketing groups. He eventually landed a job with the William Morris Agency in Los Angeles as a book analyst and story consultant for five years.

Upon leaving Los Angeles, he returned to his family home in Pennsylvania, where he turned his writing efforts toward personal interests. He's written several books and three screenplays, and continues to focus on new projects, including a novel and a historical book based on the exploits of an ancestor who'd been captured by a native Pennsylvania tribe during the Revolutionary War. In his spare time, he enjoys bicycling, motorcycling, hiking and camping in the northwestern Pennsylvania wilds.